LOOPS

LOOPS

Building Products with Clarity & Confidence

J CORNELIUS

LIONCREST
PUBLISHING

LOOPS
Building Products with Clarity & Confidence

ISBN   978-1-5445-0363-9 *Hardcover*
      978-1-5445-0362-2 *Paperback*
      978-1-5445-0361-5 *Ebook*

To my wonderful wife, Stacey, who keeps me sane; our kids who keep me curious; all the wonderful people who work at Nine Labs, who keep me motivated; and last but not least, all the clients we've had the pleasure of working with, who keep us learning.

CONTENTS

INTRODUCTION

"Follow the path of the unsafe, independent thinker. Expose your ideas to the danger of controversy. Speak your mind and fear less the label of 'crackpot' than the stigma of conformity."

THOMAS J. WATSON, FORMER CEO AND CHAIRMAN, IBM

Have you ever had a brilliant idea? Maybe you thought of an app that would make your life easier. Maybe you thought of a way to improve something you already use. Maybe you work in a big company, and you're just trying to make things better. Most people have had these types of ideas. What happens next?

Did you try to build it? Did you build a company around it? My guess is you started working on that idea in your mind's eye and got stuck somewhere along the way. Don't beat yourself up. That happens a lot.

People get stuck because they don't have a simple framework for building things people love. Building things is hard and messy. Lots of people think it's a linear process, with one step after another. After all, that's how we go through life, one step at a time.

Building great products is a messy and convoluted process that can feel confusing until you see the patterns that help make sense of it all. This book is intended to do just that—make sense of the chaos. Over the last twenty-five years, I've seen patterns that can increase the clarity and confidence you need to build great products.

I call these patterns "Loops." More on that later.

A QUICK STORY

When I was six years old, my mom gave me a remote-controlled G.I. Joe tank for Christmas. We were poor, and she probably spent a whole week's pay on it. It was the coolest thing I'd ever seen. After a few minutes of proudly driving it around the living room—crashing over the discarded wrapping paper, bows, and boxes—I got curious about what made the turret turn and how the tracks worked. So I went back to my bedroom and took the whole thing apart.

Sometime later, Mom found me like a skilled mechanic

disassembling an engine. I'd laid out all the parts of this tank in nice, neat rows and groups. Every screw and tiny part arranged and accounted for. I was thrilled. She was not. Here I was, this little kid with his new toy all in pieces across the bedroom floor. Needless to say, she chastised me for "breaking" something she'd spent a lot of money on. I told her it would be okay, but she wasn't buying it. Then an hour or so later, I drove the fully functional tank back into the living room and explained how it worked to my astonished mother.

I've always been curious about how things work. I'm constantly thinking about the mechanics behind people's motivations, about the incentives and disincentives in the systems that drive behavior. When I look at great business models, I ask myself what makes them work. When businesses fail, I want to know why.

When I started my first business out of high school, I was that six-year-old boy disassembling a tank again. I was in over my head, and it took lots of effort to figure out how things worked. But I did it anyway. Over the last twenty-five years, I've taken things apart and put them back together again many times. I've grown five companies and built literally hundreds of software products, systems, platforms, and services. Now I'm taking what I've learned and driving the tank back into the living room. But instead of my mom, this time I'm explaining how it works to you.

SO, YOU WANT TO MAKE SOMETHING GREAT?

You probably picked this book up hoping to get practical tips and tricks to help you make better products and services. The good news? Those tips and tricks are in here. The bad news? Creating something of real value takes changing how you think about what you're making and who you're making it for. It also takes a lot of work. It's messy, challenging, rewarding, complicated, and surprisingly simple at the same time. Lots of people either overthink things and make it too complex, or take shortcuts when things get hard and miss crucial steps. This book should help you strike a balance and learn how to do things right with the appropriate amount of effort.

Creating a product or service people love is hard work, but the reward of seeing people use (and pay for) the thing you made is completely worth it. Whether you're building something new or breathing new life into something that already exists, the concepts, exercises, and activities in this book will help you create something great.

First, let's reset the way you think about products.

THE NEW ECONOMY

In the dark ages before the Internet, we lived in a *seller-driven economy*. People were only aware of what was at their local market, so they had limited choices. People relied on advertising and word of mouth to learn about new products and services. Companies would create new products based on not much more than a Don Draper-esque hunch and a few focus groups, then blast them into the world with very little targeting by today's standards. Companies could succeed through the sheer brute force of mass marketing and advertising. If Gillette made a new razor, people who need razors would likely buy it because of how often they saw it advertised and how few competing products there were on shelves.

In this seller-driven economy, reaching a mass market was really only possible for large companies like Unile-ver, Procter & Gamble, and Coca-Cola that could spend millions on national advertising campaigns. Today, some startup down the street can make a Google ad in five min-utes that can reach a huge (and highly targeted) audience for a fraction of that cost. And that's not even counting all the ways to reach people on social media. Just look at how rapidly Dollar Shave Club has grown, gobbling up Gillette's market share with a fraction of their advertising budget. Now you see Gillette offering razor subscriptions to compete with the little guy. This wouldn't have been possible without the power of the Internet.

The Internet has given consumers access to nearly any product, anywhere in the world, at any time. This access to the "long tail" of products and services has shifted the landscape and created a *buyer-driven economy*. People now have access to niche products which satisfy their specific wants and needs. As this trend continues and more options become available to buyers, sellers face increased pressure to create products that people will not only buy and use but actually love.

The good news is the Internet has also given companies access to previously invisible groups of customers. The long tail goes both ways.

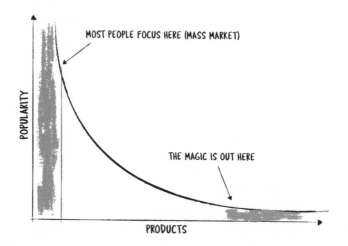

The challenge is no longer finding and reaching your customers—it's understanding them. What are their needs and wants, pains and fears? To build a successful business, you must intimately understand your customers because they are the ones driving today's economy forward. Don't be afraid to get really specific about who your target customer is. With the tools and techniques you'll learn in the following pages, coupled with the power of modern advertising and social media platforms, you'll be able to describe who they are, find them, and build things for them with amazing results. As we like to say, there are riches in the niches.

WHY HUMAN-CENTERED DESIGN MATTERS

This shift to a buyer-driven economy has increased the need for human-centered design, or what some academics call *customer centricity*, which means creating products with your customers in mind. Companies that blindly mass produce products for a loosely defined market are a relic of the pre-Internet days. Companies who don't make the shift to human-centered thinking will go the way of the Tyrannosaurus Rex—once mighty, now merely a fossil. The companies thriving today provide value with products tailor-made to deliver value for their customers. Note: this doesn't mean you have to make each product for each customer by hand. That doesn't scale. It simply means you're focused on creating value at a very personal level. Mass customization should not be confused with custom-made.

In order to create products that are valuable to people, you have to understand their **needs, wants,** and **fears.**

When you understand your customer, you can make magic happen.

Take shoes for example. People *need* shoes. Above that, people *want* shoes that will make them feel good, help them perform a task, or maybe even be a bit more stylish. If people have a *fear* about shoes (outside of a basic expectation of quality), it's buying ones that don't fit right, fail to match their personal style, or don't perform as expected.

Nike understands this, which is why they launched NIKEiD, an online lab of sorts for creating personalized shoes. If I want blue sneakers with orange laces and J Cornelius on the side in bold letters, Nike will let me build those shoes and ship them directly to my house. No trip to the mall necessary. This is a massive shift from the mass-market sneakers that made Nike one of the most recognized brands in the world.

Nike became a multibillion-dollar company because they designed and sold shoes that people loved wearing. They didn't have to offer customizable shoes when they've provided value at a macro level for over fifty years now. But Nike understands that in a buyer-driven economy, tremendous value can be found in serving customers at the *micro* level. Nike earned an estimated $100 million in revenue from NIKEiD alone in 2009, and now Nike's direct-to-consumer sales are estimated to be nearly 35 percent of their overall revenue. Human-centered business clearly drives results.

A LITTLE CUSTOMIZATION GOES A LONG WAY

Now that the Internet has unlocked the long tail of products and services, today's customers expect products built to address their wants and needs. The one-size-fits-all approach that worked fifty years ago is no longer enough to keep customers happy. Companies that aren't willing or able to provide value at the individual level will be swept out the door by competitors that will give buyers the customized offerings they want.

I'm not saying every product has to be tailor-made for each individual. What I am saying is that a little customization can go a long way toward creating value in your customer's eyes, the kind of value that makes them choose your product or service over your competition.

Take Zappos for example. Their mobile app lets people customize their shopping experience with lots of different filters. You can search by color, brand, style, size, and many other options. What's most interesting is you can *exclude* products of a certain color, style, or brand from search results. This makes it a lot easier to browse and explore options you might not know exist while ignoring things you know you *don't* want, which is more like shopping in a physical store. This might seem like a small feature, but it helps shoppers find the stuff they're looking for faster. It also illustrates one of the core reasons people choose to buy through Zappos. It's easier and more personalized than other options.

When they first launched, Zappos's primary value was offering free shipping and free returns, but today you can get that service from lots of online or brick-and-mortar stores. The value Zappos gives people—what keeps them coming back—is an easier way to buy shoes and other things. They addressed the *gains* people want—wide selection, great service, competitive price—and addressed the *pains* people have—time spent browsing physical stores, difficulty finding desired products, cost of shipping and returns. In case you forgot, Zappos was acquired by Amazon for $1.2 billion. It's another example of a human-centered business delivering massive results.

THERE IS NO FINISH LINE WITH DESIGN

I wrote this book to be a template for human-centered business design. In the chapters to come, you'll find a proven process that will help you work through the challenges of launching a new business or adding a new product to your existing lineup.

My company, Nine Labs, has used this process to create hundreds of software applications, start dozens of businesses, and transform countless companies. Though I'm mainly talking about building software, apps, and tech companies (and I consider Dollar Shave Club a tech company), I'll use the word "product" throughout this book for simplicity's sake. The thing to remember is this process applies to building anything you want or starting any kind of business, be it an app, a website, a service, or even physical products!

Now if you're envisioning a finish line with this process (like the end of the book), we should adjust your way of thinking before getting started. Human-centered business design is an iterative process that never stops. It's presented here in a linear fashion, but in reality, it's more like a series of Loops. As long as you run your business, you'll constantly move back and forth between these Loops because "design" is not a noun. It's a verb.

Design is the process of moving something from your mind's eye into reality.

Even if you're not creating new products, you'll continuously work through these Loops to refine and improve the products you already offer. Put simply, the design process is never finished.

FALL IN LOVE WITH THE PROBLEM, NOT THE SOLUTION

It's also important to know before you move forward that success with this process hinges on you being in love with the problem you're trying to solve, not the solution you create.

A few years ago, a bright-eyed entrepreneur came to me with an idea for a new app to help people accomplish their goals by saving more money. Saving enough money is a big problem in the US, so I took the meeting. That's when it got weird.

They wanted people to recommend stores and restaurants which were offering coupons, then split the savings between the person who recommended the store and the person who went there. Nobody actually received money. Instead, users earned credits that could be redeemed for discounts at other stores in the system.

The entrepreneur thought stores would want to participate because people would come in to use the credits they earned, and people would participate to earn credits for use in these stores. At no point did the business model actually address the core problem: *putting money in savings!* It was a confusing and convoluted business model with absolutely no market validation. When I suggested they go talk to people about the pains and gains of saving money, they scoffed and said, "This will work, I just know it!" Three years later, that entrepreneur hasn't built anything and is still looking for funding.

If you want to create a product with the best chance of solving the problem you've identified, and you want to make money doing it, this book will help you. If you're determined to build that million-dollar idea you've come up with and force-feed it to the market, this book is not for you. Furthermore, I'd think twice about starting a business with this mindset.

History is littered with entrepreneurs whose businesses failed because they pursued the wrong solution even when the evidence and their customers pointed them in a different direction.

You have to stay focused on the problem because the solution may be something you can't quite see yet or never expected in the first place. You have to be willing to go where the evidence leads you and listen to what customers tell you, even if they're ripping your "perfect" solution to shreds.

When I tell business owners this, they'll often come back with the famous Steve Jobs line: "A lot of times, people don't know what they want until you show it to them."

What they don't realize is that when you look at the context of that quote, yes, Jobs was talking about the iPod, but he was really talking about solving a problem. He didn't see that people wanted a white block with a spinning wheel for the controls. He saw people wanted an easier way to play music. Jobs and the team at Apple validated the problem and then built a product to solve it. He exemplified the idea of falling in love with the problem, not the solution.

Of course, we all know what a success the iPod and then the iPhone, after it, have been. These products essentially reshaped the music, telephony, and personal computing industries for good. Human-centered design wins again.

APPLYING AN OLD PROCESS IN A NEW WAY

Not too long ago, I was meeting with a client, and a colleague named Rachel mentioned that she was born in 1989, which was the same year I started my first business. I made the joke that "my career is exactly one Rachel old."

In that moment, I was reminded of how long I've been doing this. I've seen business owners struggle with the same problems for three decades now. Although my office is filled with books that dance around how to solve those problems, none of them fully do.

This book is intended to be a cohesive template that

stitches everything together in a way that makes sense for somebody who, unlike myself, doesn't do this every day.

There are many other people who could have written this book. For whatever reason, they haven't (or at least not in the same way), so this book is my attempt to fill a need that I see. I want to give my team at Nine Labs and all the other teams like us a template for how we can help our clients succeed, and I want to give you, the reader, a tool to build products and businesses focused on the right things so you can succeed too.

As you work through the processes described in this book, you'll realize that they're processes humans have done intuitively for centuries. What I've done is apply them to problems today's business owners and executives face, those at the intersection of business, design, and technology. The solutions to these problems aren't always obvious, but they are easier to find when you know what to look for and how to find it.

I WANT TO HELP YOU GET IT RIGHT

Whether by luck or by intuition, I've used these processes for a long time and built numerous companies and products. I've experienced a lot of success and plenty of failure. When I look back at those times we failed, it was when we didn't do something in this process the right way. The times that we succeeded were when we got all the steps right.

That's why I'm writing this book: I want to help *you* get it right, to avoid wasting time and money creating products that nobody wants to use. I can't promise you that this journey will be easy or straightforward or that you'll become the next Jeff Bezos. I can guarantee that your chances of success increase the more you buy into this process and trust that it will produce the results you want.

If you're ready, let's start by diving into the specifics of human-centered business design to better understand why it's the best way to build a company in today's world.

SHOULD WE DO IT?

You probably get ideas all the time, and a lot of ideas seem good at the time you have them. A few ideas turn out to be good, a few of those turn into products, and even fewer turn into viable businesses. The difference between the ones that make it and the ones that don't is simple: market/product fit. Some of you might be thinking, "Wait, isn't it *product/market fit?*" I like to reverse that and put the market first since that keeps us focused on the problem we're solving first. The people who go out into the market and find a group of customers who have a problem—*and are willing to pay to get it solved*—are the people who end up building successful businesses.

The people who simply fall in love with their idea and never try to validate it will go around in circles because they haven't found a market. They haven't found their tribe. But the people who *fall in love with the problem*—and not their idealized solution—are the people who are most likely to succeed.

This first phase is fundamental to everything else you will do in building a business. It is the cornerstone. But don't let the name "Phase One" fool you. This is a continuous journey that never ends. You will *always* be talking to customers to discover their problems and pain points, and what they're willing to pay to have them solved.

You have to find the market of people who are willing to pay to solve a problem before you can actually build a business. If you can't do that, you need to get comfortable with the reality that your idea probably isn't worth pursuing. You might be able to have a hobby, but you can't build a scalable business.

We're interested in building products people want. Let's start off by answering the first question of human-centered business design: *Should we do it?*

Chapter One

HUMAN-CENTERED BUSINESS DESIGN

"Entrepreneurs are moving from a world of problem-solving to a world of problem-finding. The very best ones are able to uncover problems people didn't realize that they had."

DANIEL PINK

In order to understand what people want, we first have to understand how they make decisions. Understanding how people make decisions requires a little brain science. Don't worry. This won't hurt.

ANALYSIS PARALYSIS

Have you ever fallen victim to analysis paralysis? I bet you have. Not sure what that is? Here's an example:

You're in the condiments aisle of your local grocer looking at thirty different jars of jelly. Some say "Organic" on the label, while others have obscene amounts of sugar. You narrow your search for the perfect jelly down to the ones that are organic, then toss out the overpriced options. Now you have eleven choices that all seem equally good—how do you decide which one to pick?

If you're like most people, you might get frustrated and walk away without jelly because you have no good way of choosing between the final eleven options. Or you might get frustrated and just grab the jar with the most attractive label or lowest price, disregarding the quality of ingredients. After all, why devote that much time, effort, and attention to a choice that has very little impact on your life?

The same thing happens when you're on the pricing page for some online service and are trying to decide which plan to subscribe to. Having too many options or not being able to clearly tell the difference between them will leave you paralyzed. Not signing up today!

When our brains are forced to make too many tiny decisions, it can shut us down. This is analysis paralysis, and it happens all the time. When people don't have clear and compelling information to base decisions on, they will choose not to decide and just walk away.

MAKING DECISIONS BASED IN FEAR

Let's look at another stumbling block to decision-making: *fear*.

It's generally pretty easy to choose which pair of socks to wear in the morning because there's not much risk involved in that choice. Nobody really cares if you wear the blue socks or the green socks (unless you're the type who matches socks to the rest of your outfit).

But when it comes to changing your bank, there's a high level of fear involved. You might be incredibly frustrated with your bank, but you won't switch because the process is too complex and there's a chance something could go wrong. Most people, especially those living paycheck to paycheck, can't risk having something go wrong and losing money.

The rewards of such a move also don't outweigh the risks. An extra 1 percent interest on a savings account is not worth the pain and aggravation of doing all the paperwork.

So people hardly ever change banks...and banks know that.

THE LIZARD BRAIN AT WORK

These are just two simple examples of how people make decisions, rational or not, based on basic brain science. We start our discussion of human-centered business design here because making products that people love to use begins with understanding the human brain.

As we just saw, our brains can put up barriers that keep us from acting. If your product makes customers think too much or sparks fear or uncertainty, it's dead on arrival.

The fear response comes from the low-functioning part of our brain, lovingly referred to as the "lizard brain." This part of the brain only understands two things: fear and desire.

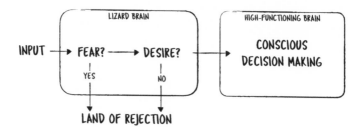

The lizard brain first evaluates everything you see, every time you see it. Here's how:

FEAR: Is this safe? Should I be afraid of this thing? Is it going to hurt me?

Get past the fear gatekeeper, and you've got a chance. The next hurdle is this:

DESIRE: If it's not dangerous, is it desirable?

If I desire it, how? Do I want to eat it? Mate with it? Own it?

This all stems from our evolutionary survival instincts, and we can't avoid it no matter how hard we try. Think about this: if someone you trust points a gun at your head, you're going to be uncomfortable. Your more developed brain— the one that trusts that person—can't override the fear response coming from the lizard brain. You're probably a little uncomfortable even thinking about that situation. That's how powerful the lizard brain is. We can't ignore the lizard brain, but we can figure out how to get past it.

GETTING PAST THE LIZARD BRAIN

If you check those first two boxes, the decision will go up to your more developed brain, which has two distinct parts: the *slow-thinking brain* and the *fast-thinking brain*.

The *slow brain* is where we do more long-term and complicated thinking. It's what most of us would call our subconscious. When you have that idea that comes out of nowhere in the shower, that's your *slow brain* feeding something it's been working on up to your *fast brain*. Also, you know when you want to "sleep on it"? That's your *fast brain* handing something off to the *slow brain* for processing.

The *fast brain* is what you're using right now to process the words on this page and turn them into thoughts inside your head. It's what you use to talk, do math, drive a car, play sports (to some degree), and many people agree this is where most decisions get made.

For more about the fast and slow brains, I recommend you read *Thinking, Fast and Slow* by Daniel Kahneman and *Hare Brain, Tortoise Mind* by Guy Claxton.

Back to making that decision. After something gets past the lizard brain, it moves up to the high-functioning brain where we make "educated" decisions. But if your product gets slapped down by the lizard brain customers won't—scratch that—*can't* buy it because the decision to purchase never reached their high-functioning brain!

FEAR AND DESIRE

Remember, the lizard brain only understands two things: *fear* and *desire,* in that order. So to get past the lizard brain, we have to *avoid triggering fear.* Some fears are primal and universal: fear of being hurt or dying, fear of running out of food (see fear of dying), fear of losing something we value, like money, status, friends, or love.

There are many great books about all the things people are afraid of, so I won't go into more detail here. Just know there are a lot of things people fear, and knowing what the people in your target market fear will help you avoid being discarded by the lizard brain. If all you do is focus on the *fear of loss* (in all the ways it presents itself), you'll be far ahead of your competitors who aren't thinking this way at all.

Just because you haven't triggered fear doesn't mean you're good to go. Your product still has to be *desirable.* Products that don't trigger fear and don't create desire are generally just overlooked. You might have what you think is secret sauce, but your target market just sees ketchup.

To be desirable, you have to understand what your target market *needs* and *wants.* You should be creating a product that satisfies those needs and wants while avoiding the fear response.

If the desire is strong enough, it can cause us to act, even if we have no incentive to do so. If you show me a shirt that's my favorite color, style, and is on sale, I will seriously think about buying it because it's desirable to me, even though I don't *need* another shirt.

DANGEROUS TERRITORY

You can also get past the fear response by being desirable even if your product triggers fear! Think about a roller coaster. The desire for a thrill is so powerful that it overwhelms the sense of fear or danger that a roller coaster elicits in our lizard brain.

Like we talked about in the introduction, you're much more likely to create products that are valuable to people when you deeply understand their needs, wants, and fears.

By getting past the fear response and appearing desirable, it's possible to transform a want into a need. People need food, but they want ice cream because it's desirable.

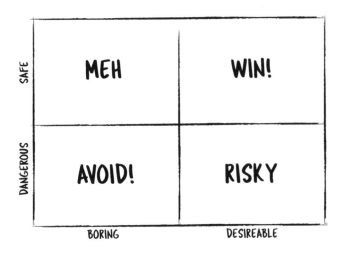

Right now you might be thinking, "This is all interesting, but what does it have to do with building products?" Bear with me. All this psychology is actually really important to how we make design decisions. It'll all make sense soon. Keep reading.

EXCHANGE THEORY

The interplay between these three factors of needs, wants, and fears affects the *perceived value* of your product. Which is hugely important because it plays into how people decide what to pay. This is what's known as *exchange theory*. Here's the gist: if the perceived value of your product is greater than its perceived cost, people will buy it. If the perceived cost is greater than the perceived value, they won't buy it. It's really that simple.

Value > Cost = Yes

Cost > Value = No

The key word here is *perceived*.

Value and cost involve more than just money. There's a time consideration: Does the product save me time, or does it take a long time to use effectively? There's the impact a product has on our reputation: if a product will make you look cool, professional, or smart, its perceived value goes way up. When Kanye West designed a plain, white T-shirt and sold it for $120, people bought it because they wanted to own the "Kanye shirt" even though they probably knew it was a bad economic decision.

On the other hand, if owning or using a certain product makes you feel embarrassed or out of style, the perceived value will plummet. Flip phones fell off hard when smartphones came out, didn't they?

Opportunity cost also plays a role in the buying decision. If Joe buys your $1,000 television, what will he not be able to buy as a result? Opportunity cost is not directly reflected in your product's price, but it absolutely affects its perceived cost.

Exchange theory affects every transaction people do.

Think about it. Will you spend $99 on something when there's a nearly identical product right next to it for $97? Maybe. What if it were $79? Will you spend time to go to a store to get a product if you don't really need it? Probably not. The price of that thing might not be the problem, but the time and effort required to get it are. (This is how Amazon beats your local store with the same product.) Would you buy a product you know you need—let's say an email marketing service—if you're unsure if it will have all the features you need? Probably not.

You might think your product is exactly what a customer needs, but unless they can perceive the value they'll receive and see the value is greater than the cost, it won't matter.

COGNITIVE BIASES

To understand why humans make certain decisions, seek to understand their biases. I've recently been working with a startup that helps people who operate airports on a large scale. The work the airport employees do is extremely stressful. In developing Value Propositions with the startup, we found what's most important to the airport employees isn't necessarily doing their job better. Instead, it's making sure their peers understand what they are doing. If employees don't have the confidence of their peers, then their peers won't follow protocol, which could cause all kinds of problems.

Even if these airport employees would be better served by tangible changes, like better documentation or a more effective communication channel, they would find the greatest value in being better understood by their colleagues.

This is an emotional response tied to their bias that greater understanding will lead to more cooperation and better results. Right or wrong, this bias affects how they act. This insight led to a major shift in how they talked about and built their product, which led to a rapid increase in adoption and revenue. Human-centered design wins again.

When you understand the motivations behind the decisions your customers make, you'll have a better idea of how to tap into those motivations and create real value for them.

ARE YOU SPEAKING TO THE RIGHT AUDIENCE?

Let's see how exchange theory and cognitive biases interact with a quick case study. On one side, you have a teenage girl; on the other, a successful Wall Street broker. They both have the same objective: buy a new outfit. How will their approaches differ?

One motivation for the teenage girl is status. She wants

an outfit that looks good, fits well, and signals certain characteristics to others (cute, stylish, edgy, preppy, etc.). Another motivation is cost. She doesn't have a lot of money, so she's bargain shopping. What she's not worried about is time. She'll put aside homework, chores, and even hanging out with friends to hit up every store until she finds the perfect outfit. For her, time is worth less than money, so she bases her decisions accordingly.

Turn now to the Wall Street broker. She's also motivated by status. In her world, a $10,000 suit is expected attire. If she doesn't wear one, it might signal to her peers that she doesn't belong. Unlike the young girl, she is worried about time. Every minute of her day is scheduled; there's no time for shopping. What the broker doesn't care about is money. She'll happily pay $10,000 to a tailor who will measure her for fit, then design and deliver the suit when it's ready.

The teenage girl and the Wall Street broker did the same thing: they bought an outfit. They even had the same underlying motivation: fitting in with their peers. However, they took different approaches because their values were different.

Imagine if you designed an app that helped users pick out clothes the way the teenage girl did by taking lots of time to look at all the options, then marketed it to Wall Street brokers. Would you get many people recommending it, much less any repeat business? Unlikely.

THE SUNK COST FALLACY

Another psychological phenomenon worth mentioning here (but for different reasons) is the *sunk cost fallacy*, which we've all fallen victim to at some point. It's the idea that because we've put so much time, money, or effort into something that's gone poorly, we must see it through in hopes that finishing it will make the outcome better. We rationalize investing even more time and money by saying if we give up, our investment won't pay off. That's the wrong mindset. In truth, when things are going sideways, the investment you made will probably never pay off.

I say this now because you need to understand that, like the entrepreneur who wanted people to swap coupons for credits as a way to save money, just chasing an idea with no market validation is a terrible idea.

Let's say you have to invest $1,000 a month for one year, and you have to sell the investment at the end of the year. You decide to buy $1,000 of a company's stock each month. In January, the stock is $37 per share. It rises a little through the summer, and things are looking good, but come November, the stock is in the toilet at $12 per share, and you've lost a significant amount of money. Would you throw in the final $1,000 just to see things through, knowing you had to sell it all a month later? Only if you were insane or just loved wasting money. With an objective measure of the performance of that investment, putting another $1,000 in would be nuts. Yet some people, like our coupon-saving friend, will keep investing in a bad idea even when they're not seeing any returns.

When you're trying to build a new company, you don't always have that objective measure at first. But when you find it, you can't ignore it. This goes back to falling in love with the problem, not the solution. If your solution isn't accepted within some reasonable amount of time, you must try to find another one.

Look, nobody wants to be told that their baby is ugly. But I'm here to tell you it's a mistake to keep searching for the one customer who will buy your product. So many entrepreneurs think their customer is out there waiting to be found. The mistake here is that you are investing in something you never validated. You haven't proven if other people actually want your product! If you keep pushing, you'll blow through all your money and have nothing to use for the next big idea.

Now, let's get back to talking about your idea.

AN IDEA VS. A HUNCH

Let's start putting these ideas into action. How do you begin to build a product that people will love, one that can support an entire business? It starts with an idea.

An idea usually begins with the question: "I wonder if this will work?"

Ideas are great. It's safe to say millions of business ideas are born every day. However, it's important to remember that **ideas are worthless without execution**. An idea is the seed from which everything grows, but a seed by itself won't grow into anything. It needs effort to make it grow.

You need an idea with some velocity. You need a hunch. With a hunch, you say to yourself, "I think this will work, I'm going to do it."

A hunch is actionable. It gives you direction. You move from having an idea to a hunch when you see some proof that your idea might be useful to other people. Don't spend time trying to turn your idea into a business. Work on turning your idea into a hunch. The first step is asking yourself a few questions.

1. **Inevitable?** Is there any version of the future where this does not exist? If so, what is that future and how likely is it?

2. **Solvable?** This one is tricky. It's really easy to let your bias and bravado fool you into thinking it's solvable. Be super honest with yourself and talk to other people about it. If so, do any solutions already exist?
3. **Recognizable?** When you talk about the idea with other people, do they recognize the problem or need?
4. **Verifiable?** If you actually solve this problem, how will you measure that you've done it? How will you know?

It's time to start doing research, talking with people about your hunch, and validating that people have the problem you want to solve (we'll look at this in-depth in the next chapter). You may not know what the solution is yet, but that's okay.

THE SOLUTION IS YOUR DESTINATION

It's easy to fly from New York to London as a passenger. You get on the plane, listen to the announcements, order a drink, watch a couple movies, and then land in London. It's all very uneventful.

That same flight from New York to London is a totally different experience in the cockpit. Up there, the pilot is constantly adjusting due to changing weather conditions, talking with air traffic control, and keeping an eye on the plane's instruments. Over the course of the flight, the pilot might make 9,000 or 10,000 tiny adjustments to the flight path to land safely in London. If the pilot just kept blindly flying in the exact same direction, the plane might end up in Africa or at the North Pole!

The process of human-centered business design is similar. As you do research, every tiny bit of information you get is going to adjust your course a little. Every person you speak to may shift your process a minuscule amount, and you have to listen to that. Be open to making those course corrections, or you are going to end up way off target.

Oh, and you're flying blind. You have no idea where London is. The customers will tell you where they think London is. The truth is London exists somewhere between all the truth you hear from your customers. Your job is to map it out and find it, kind of like a treasure hunt. You'll have to experiment with your flight path, and perhaps you'll fall off course a bit, but you can touch base with your customers and figure out if you're on the right path. If you want to succeed, you have to be willing to listen to those people and let your path be dictated for you. You can't predetermine it.

Your destination isn't a product (not yet). Your destination is the solution.

WHAT CAN YOU BE GREAT AT?

When you understand the needs, wants, and fears of your customer, you can deliver them something of value. In the same way, there are three forces that determine how successful the business that you build around that product will be:

- Product quality: How good is the product?
- Operational efficiency: How good are you at making and delivering the product?
- Customer heterogeneity: How customized is the product?

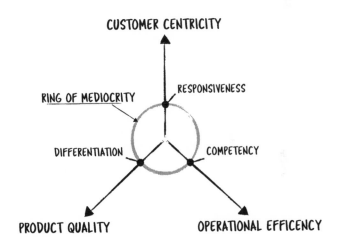

As you can see, these three forces pull on one another, which makes it very difficult to excel in all three categories. To survive, you need to be great in at least one area and at least average in the other two. If you manage to be great in all three, you're likely a billion-dollar business (as we'll see).

Take Campbell's soup for example. They have a very high operational efficiency, churning out millions of cans of soup. Their product is also pretty good quality. But there's no customization. If you want Campbell's minestrone soup, but you don't want chickpeas in it, you're out of luck. You get what's in the can, and that's it. There's no customization.

No one would argue that Campbell's isn't a successful company, but that's because they're great in one area (operational efficiency) and good in another (product quality). If they churned out cans of terrible tasting soup, they'd be out of business. Even without the customization, they're doing enough in the other two areas to be a profitable business.

On the other end of the spectrum, look at a custom jeweler. They might produce a superb level of *product quality* because they've been making jewelry by hand for decades and are highly skilled. The jeweler also has a very high level of *customer heterogeneity* because they are making precisely what the customer wants. But the jeweler's *operational efficiency* is very low. A single jeweler who creates high-quality, customized products cannot create thousands of them in a year.

Finally, let's look at the iPhone. It's a beautiful, high-quality product. Apple obviously has high operational efficiency: they make a lot of iPhones, very quickly, at a high level of quality. The *customer heterogeneity* side is where it gets interesting.

The device itself, the hardware, is not customizable other than a few color options for the case. But that doesn't matter. You can customize every aspect of how you use it. You can install your own apps and arrange them however you want. You can change every setting however you like all the way down to your ringtone or wallpaper. You can buy a colorful case and install one of those handle type things that go on the back so you don't drop your phone. This is very high *customer heterogeneity*.

This goes back to what we covered in the introduction: a little customization can go a long way. Your iPhone might be the same as your neighbor's, but if you both placed your phones on a table, you could still tell them apart. Apple doesn't make custom phones, but by offering little ways to make your phone stand out, they scratch that itch for customization.

Apple has nailed all three axes of the chart. The fact their products have high *customer heterogeneity*, AND they're great at *product quality* and *operational efficiency* makes them one of the world's most valuable companies.

HOW TO ADAPT TO CHANGING EXPECTATIONS

The buyer-driven economy has shifted the importance of customer heterogeneity. More than ever, you need to ask yourself: How can I customize what I offer my customers?

Look at Amazon, which took years to turn its first net profit in 2001. Since then, they've become one of the most profitable companies in the world. Why? Their operational efficiency is unmatched, yet for the most part (save for Kindle and Alexa devices, and Amazon Basics), they don't make many physical products. Their primary product *is* their service. They have a vast selection of almost everything you can imagine, and they've made it no-brainer simple to order and buy from them. They've also eliminated the fear and uncertainty around shipping costs with Amazon Prime and a liberal return policy. Even the hardware devices they make are geared to get you to buy more stuff. It's a beautiful business model, and their financials prove it.

Use me as an example: I like to barbecue, so I have a charcoal subscription through Amazon. Sounds silly, right? Every five weeks, a new bag of charcoal arrives at my house. Will I ever buy charcoal any other way? Probably not. In fact, I do this with a lot of commodity products from toothpaste to air filters to dog food. Amazon has allowed me to fully customize my shopping experience and remove a lot of friction from the process. The same is true for millions of people across the world. Human-centered design wins again.

A product customized to a human automatically brings more value. If you go to a steakhouse and order a steak, but they don't ask you how you want it cooked and it comes out raw, you'll probably never go back to that steakhouse. If they do ask you how you want it cooked, and you ask for medium rare, but the steak comes out well done, you'll never go back there either. But if you go to that steakhouse, order it medium rare, and it comes exactly the way you want it every single time, you're probably going to be loyal to that steakhouse.

I'm not saying you need to be Amazon, but can you be that steakhouse? Can you offer that little bit of personalization and humanity your customers are seeking? If so, you'll quickly find them seeking out your product.

To recap:

1. An understanding of the way people make decisions should be at the center of how you think about what you want to create.
2. You need to ask yourself, is it Inevitable, Solvable, Recognizable, and Verifiable?
3. And finally, how can you ensure that you can be great

at customer heterogeneity, product quality, and operational efficiency?

Ready to get started building something your customers will love? Let's jump into the next chapter and tackle the first step of this process: research.

Chapter Two

STEP ONE: RESEARCH

"No idea survives its first encounter with a customer."

STEVE BLANK

You're probably familiar with Mailchimp. It's an all-in-one marketing platform used by millions of customers all over the world to send billions of emails every month. What you might not know is that Mailchimp's roots stretch back to a website consulting agency called Rocket Science Group. A number of RSG's customers all had the same problem: they wanted a reliable way to send emails that looked good regardless of the recipient's email provider.

At the time, most email was viewed via Outlook or Gmail, which had drastically different ways of displaying an email. You could send something that looked great in Gmail, but it might look terrible in Outlook. Plus, Gmail and Outlook weren't the only email platforms around.

Platforms like Lotus Notes, Yahoo Mail, Hotmail, and AOL were also widely used, and each of them had their oddities about how to display an email.

Because Rocket Science Group heard the same problem from a lot of their customers, their idea (people need a way to reliably send good-looking emails) evolved into a hunch. To test their hunch, they built a simple tool that allowed customers to send templated emails. Customers loved it so much that Rocket Science Group launched Mailchimp to keep the momentum going and find the best solution to this problem.

It all started when the co-founders validated a problem by listening to their customers. They didn't assume that everyone had this problem when a small group of people did—they validated it through multiple conversations with customers.

We'll follow Mailchimp's journey throughout each chapter to see how they worked through the process of human-centered business design. Without knowing it—since this process wasn't fully articulated in the early 2000s—they followed the steps we'll cover in this book, the first of which is research. They talked to customers to validate the problem they were trying to solve, flesh out who had this problem, and develop confidence that they were on the right track pursuing a solution to this problem for these people. Mailchimp still conducts research into their customers' needs every day. In fact, top executives still visit mom-and-pop customers on a regular basis to make sure they stay in tune with what people want.

THE PROBLEM DISCOVERY PROCESS

The research phase is all about building confidence, which starts with knowing the problem you want to research. At this point, you're in one of two groups: the problem you want to solve is clear, or the problem you want to solve is still a bit of a mystery.

If you're confident that you know which problem you want to solve, you can skip to the section about the research framework if you want. That said, it might be worth your time to go through this problem discovery process. Here's why: you might be a *tiny bit wrong* in your assumptions. In my experience with people who go through this process, most of the time, they discover the problem is slightly different than what they originally thought.

If you don't yet have a clear problem you want to solve (or want to fine tune yours), these next two sections will help you find a problem that a significant group of people have. By taking notes on what you observe, you'll begin to develop the demographics of who is having this problem. These demographics will be refined later, but you should be able to describe your target audience in broad terms, like age, profession, location, income, education level, and more.

Let's start with the first strategy: a Problem Safari.

PROBLEM SAFARI

Much like an African safari, where you observe animals in their natural habitat, here you're going to observe problems people are having in the real world. The best place to start is with a topic that you know well or with a group of people you have access to. The topic could be anything from running to cooking to parenting, accounts receivable reconciliation to jet propulsion. The group of people you have access to could be realtors, accountants, or single moms. It doesn't really matter. All types of people doing all types of jobs have problems to solve. The key is to pick a subject you're interested in exploring at a deeper level throughout the research phase.

Starting with a broad subject will help you pick the right "watering hole," a place where people gather to discuss what they're doing or working on. It could be an athletic club, a bar, a social media group, or a subreddit. Again, it doesn't really matter where it is or what form it's in. What matters is enough similar people go there and discuss what they're doing in life.

Once you've identified the best watering holes for your subject, hang out in them and observe people. Become a member, hang around, and pay attention to what people are saying. As problems start to pop up in conversation, take good notes in a little notebook, spreadsheet, or even a napkin. How you capture notes isn't important as long as you write down the problems you hear discussed and how often they're mentioned. As you do this, you'll see patterns and themes start to emerge.

It could take a few days or a few months to get a good data set. It depends on the activity level of the community you're observing. If you're tracking civil engineers, for example, they'll probably post a few times a week in their online forum when they have a problem that needs to be solved. On the other hand, if you're in a Facebook group about running, you might have thousands of people complaining about their problems daily, so you'll get data a lot faster. No matter the speed, take good notes on what you observe.

The patterns and themes that emerge will point you to a specific problem that is worth more exploration. When you've identified it, it's time to jump into the conversation and ask some questions. Join an existing conversation or start your own by asking: "I've seen a lot of people ask about this problem. What have you tried?" If you've spent any time on social media, you know that people love to share their frustrations and their solutions.

When you join the conversation, you'll begin to understand more about the problem and the pain points (I'll explain the difference between a *problem* and *pain points* shortly) that people are experiencing. If someone jumps in to point out a widely used solution that you overlooked, you'll also save yourself time and money trying to figure out a problem that's already been solved.

If you'd like some help with this process, go search for "Amy Hoy Problem Safari." She's published lots of great content on the process.

OUTDATED TECH REVIEW

Another great way to discover a problem is to look at the ways outdated technology is causing friction in established companies or industries. For example, many professionals still use spreadsheets for tasks that software could help them do more easily.

If you have access to real estate brokers or outside salespeople or nurses or people in any other profession, ask them how they use spreadsheets. Are they using spreadsheets in a way they weren't designed to be used or wasting time fighting Excel to make it do what they want? If so, they might like that problem to be solved.

Think about email. We've all been included on some

out-of-control email threads. What happens to your productivity when you're fifteen emails deep and struggling to figure out what's going on? How about the dread you feel when you come back from vacation and know there are two hundred emails waiting in your inbox? Slack is a company that saw these problems around email, validated them, and developed a solution people love to use. Slack created a group chat platform which simplifies and streamlines the way teams communicate. Obviously, people like it because Slack has grown exponentially over the last few years, reaching $64 million in revenue just a few years after launch. Note: they also had massive venture capital investment that allowed them to move faster than others. But still, they found a problem, solved it in a way people valued, and the results speak for themselves. Human-centered design wins again.

The same rules from the Problem Safari apply here: take good notes, look for patterns and themes, and talk to as many people as you can to see how widespread the problem is.

THE RESEARCH FRAMEWORK

No matter which strategy you use, keep observing until you find a problem you can fall in love with. Once you have that problem identified, it's time to start interviewing people to validate what you found so far and build confidence that you're on the right track.

Before we get to the interviews, let's look at the framework and tools you'll use throughout this process. Starting here gives you a target to shoot for during interviews. You'll know what questions to ask and be better equipped to avoid biases (more on this later).

Throughout the interviews, you'll begin to gather demographic information on the people who have your problem. Most people would use this information to create a *persona*, which is a picture of your target customer that comes with a name and job title. It's a shortcut you can use when referring to the person whose problem you're trying to solve:

"Think about Tom, the forty-year-old broker who uses spreadsheets for lead follow-up."

Personas have two major problems:

1. People tend to focus too much on the details of the persona and not the problem they're trying to solve for the people the persona represents.
2. Personas can give you a limited view of what your target customer struggles with. Unless your organization has a robust, disciplined research team that

knows how to properly use personas, I would suggest a slightly different way of using the data you compile during interviews.

Instead, think of the problem you're trying to solve as a theatrical production with *actors* and *roles*. Demographic and psychographic (more on this soon) information is compiled to create a role, which is the aggregate of people who experience your problem in a certain way. Each role is defined by a common *pain point*. The people who fill these roles—the ones you'll talk to during interviews—are *actors*. Think about the seven men who've played James Bond since 1962. They're all actors playing the same role. From Sean Connery to Daniel Craig, they each brought something unique to the role, but they're all James Bond!

Look at the people you interview the same way. Who are they (actor) and what group do they belong in (role) based on how they experience the problem (pain point)?

HOW TO DEFINE ROLES AND PAIN POINTS

Here's a great example that illustrates how this all comes together. In Atlanta, there's a startup company called 2ULaundry. They deliver a bag to your house for you to fill with your dirty clothes. You tell them the bag is full, they come pick it up, wash and dry your clothes, and then deliver your clean laundry back to you. It's an elegant and well-executed solution to this problem: *I don't want to do my laundry.*

For the sake of example let's say that when 2ULaundry was validating this problem, they identified three roles that experienced this problem in unique ways (i.e., they had a specific pain point).

- The first role is working parents whose time is taken up by their work and kids' activities, so they want to outsource laundry to get back time they can use elsewhere. This role doesn't want to do laundry (problem) because they don't have time (pain point).
- The second role is successful career-types who have the time to do their laundry, but they also have enough money to not bother with the hassle of laundry. This role doesn't want to do laundry (problem) because they'd rather do something else (pain point).
- The third role are people who don't know the best way to do laundry, so now their white shirts are turning pink. This role doesn't want to do laundry (problem) because they don't know how (pain point).

All three roles have the same problem, but the way in which that problem touches their lives is different enough that 2ULaundry needs to be aware of all three roles and create Value Propositions for each of them. More on Value Propositions later.

Let's explore the research framework further by looking at one of the tools you'll use.

EMPATHY MAPS

The Empathy Map is a tool created by Dave Gray to help document and understand a specific person's perspective on completing a task. Its goal is to help us empathize with the person so we design better products for them.

You'll create an Empathy Map for each person you interview no matter what round of interviews you're on. You don't have to use this exact sheet *during* interviews; in fact, you probably shouldn't because you might run out of room while trying to take notes.

Since note-taking is so critical, you don't want to do anything that makes it more difficult to write during interviews. The important thing is to keep the structure of the Empathy Map in your mind as you talk to people. You'll use this map to distill findings from the interviews and plug your notes into each section later.

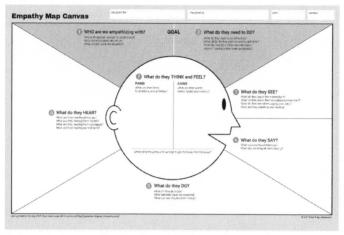

To download a copy of the Empathy Map, visit Loopsbook.com/resources.

To understand the Empathy Map, we have to understand why empathy matters. A lot of people think about empathy as this soft, squishy emotional thing.

It is emotional, but we're not trying to create a touchy-feely thing. For our purposes, we want to put ourselves in the shoes of the customer in order to objectively understand their viewpoint as much as possible.

To do that, we need to understand who they are when they're trying to accomplish a task. What do they need to do? What do they see other people doing? What do they say they are going to do? What have they actually tried? We need to understand what they observe and how they perceive the problem being solved by other people (if at all).

Stay focused on the human—the actor—who is doing this task and use the Empathy Map to document their *thoughts*, *pains*, and *gains*. Pains are things that challenge the actor or prevent them from accomplishing a task. Some example pains might be:

- It takes too long.
- I don't understand it.
- It's frustrating because it's difficult.
- I can't find the button.

Gains are what it would mean to your customer if they accomplished this task successfully or if the problem didn't exist anymore. Some examples of gains might be:

- I would get so much time back.
- I'd save so much money.
- My boss would like me.
- I'd get a promotion.

Later in the chapter, you'll see how to create an Empathy Map for each role based on the Empathy Maps you create for each actor. You'll also use the gains section of the Empathy Map in your Value Proposition Canvas. Then we'll look at the ways these gains are expressed (known as *features* and *benefits*). Don't worry about Affinity Maps or Value Proposition Canvases right now. I bring them up only to show that Empathy Maps are important because they help set up a lot of the work you'll do later.

INTERVIEW RECRUITMENT STRATEGIES

With a problem in hand and the research framework in mind, it's time to interview people! The next question, of course, is where to find interview subjects. The answer depends on whether you have a clear picture of the people with your problem (your target audience). Here are a few strategies to talk with more people and dial in your demographics a bit.

STRATEGY #1: HIT THE STREETS

For a lot of people, this is scary, but if you're brave enough to leave your office building or residence, you can gather good data just by talking to people you don't know.

If you're not comfortable approaching people on the street to ask them, for example, if they have problems with their shoelaces coming untied, head to a bar or a Starbucks and strike up conversations. Offer to buy people a drink or a coffee if they'll answer a few questions.

Sure, you might have some people tell you to buzz off, but that's okay! In my experience, if you're friendly and open, you can find enough people to happily answer your questions.

STRATEGY #2: HALLWAY TESTING

If you're not ready to get out and pound the pavement, start by talking with neighbors or people who work in your building. You'll be likely to get responses because you've probably seen these people before or even said hi to them. Again, in a friendly and open manner, tell these people you're doing some research and would like to ask them a few questions. These interviews might not provide any usable information, but it will help you get comfortable with interview tactics and be more prepared for when you're talking to someone who actually is in your target audience.

GETTING SPECIFIC

If you have a decent idea of your target audience's demographics, there are a few strategies I'd recommend to find interview subjects who match those descriptors. To start with, think about your target audience at the highest possible level and describe them:

I want to interview real estate brokers.
I want to interview college freshmen.
I want to interview women who do yoga.

For the last group, you could start by visiting yoga studios and finding popular yoga groups online. If you want to talk with college freshmen, visit a college campus. If you're worried about being the creepy person holding a clipboard, go through a campus organization to reach students who are willing to be interviewed.

To reach a group of professionals like real estate brokers, accountants, or dentists, look for professional associations in your area that have regular meetings or seek help from the local chamber of commerce. Check Meetup. com for special interest meetings or browse Facebook for groups where these professionals might hang out.

> Pro Tip: If you have some funds for research, you can run ads on Google or Craigslist, or use a website like PingPong to get help gathering interview subjects. Depending on how much money you want to spend, you can also hire a recruiting firm (not a staffing firm) for help.

No matter what round of interviews you're on, you can use these strategies to find people who match your demographics. It doesn't guarantee that all of the people you talk to will have the problem you're thinking about trying to solve, but it will help you understand more about your target market, narrow the scope of who you're trying to solve the problem for, and gather some great data about what those people think and feel. Most importantly, you'll start to understand their *needs*, *wants*, and *fears*.

THE FIRST ROUND OF INTERVIEWS

Your goal with the first round of interviews is twofold:

- Refine the demographics of your target audience
- Begin to understand and define their psychographics

Basic demographics are helpful because they help you focus on a small and specific group of people (the target market), but they provide only surface-level information. To get inside people's heads, we need more details about them.

This example shows the difference between demographics and psychographics:

Basic Demographics: Women, never married, college educated, between the ages of 28 and 34, living in the 30309 zip code, with a household income under $75,000/year, employed in a Fortune 1000 company, and who commute less than ten miles to work.

Detailed Demographics: Drive to work in a used German car, use the newest model iPhone, listen to podcasts about creativity and art, follow Ellen DeGeneres on Snapchat, post to Instagram more than five times a week (usually pictures of their dog), buy their coffee at the local coffee shop instead of Starbucks, and have a tattoo you'll probably never see.

You can see the difference, right? Basic demographics give you a rough idea of who this woman is, but the more detail we have makes that image crystal clear. That second description might even be detailed enough that somebody you know may have come to mind. That's what we're looking for. Demographics so detailed that it's hard to confuse them for someone else.

PSYCHOGRAPHICS

Ultimately, to understand the people in your target market, you need both demographics and psychographics. Psychographics are descriptors of someone's psychology, of how they make decisions. As Merriam-Webster says, "The study and classification of people according to their attitudes, aspirations, and other psychological criteria, especially in market research."

Where demographics look at things like age, income, location, education level, and employment status, psychographics look at personality, values, interests, and attitudes. You may have noticed how some of the things describing our fictional woman a few moments ago (e.g., "listen to podcasts about creativity and art") sound a bit like psychographics.

That's because they are!

What we're really trying to understand about people is how they make decisions. Are they rational, analytical, emotional, spontaneous? That type of difference and many more like it will become very important later when you're crafting your Value Propositions, so keep psychographics in mind as you're doing your interviews.

Pro Tip: Don't try to psychoanalyze people *while* you're doing the interviews. You're not trying to categorize or stereotype people. Definitely don't judge them in any way. You're just there to learn about them and their problems so you can do a better job of creating a product they'll love.

We already have the framework and the template you'll use (the Empathy Map), so let's focus our attention on doing great interviews and getting the most out of them.

INTERVIEWING HUMANS

A couple important points about interviews before we dig in. First, don't use surveys in place of interviews during the research phase. Surveys aren't ideal because people can edit what they say before they send it. Most people respond more authentically and go into more detail when you talk to them because it's easier to talk than type. When people type out responses, they tend to self-edit or self-censor, so you don't get the best answer. When people talk, the thoughts come out of their brains with less of a filter because they don't have time to go back and edit them. You want the unfiltered version of their thoughts because that's where the golden answers are.

The second word of caution ties back to something I mentioned earlier in the chapter: avoiding confirmation bias. A lot of people approach interviews with the goal of validating what they already know, so they ask questions that lead the subject to confirm their bias. Don't fall into this trap. Keep an open mind and ask the right types of questions.

PREPARING FOR YOUR INTERVIEWS

A great interview runs smoothly, and both the interviewer (you) and the interviewee feel like it was a productive conversation. You don't want your interviews to feel clumsy or to make your interviewees feel they've wasted their time.

The number one mistake most people make when doing interviews is not preparing well enough. It's not hard to prepare well, it's just most people don't know how because they've never done this before! Don't worry. I'll help you out.

SCHEDULING

A general rule to remember as you're planning your interviews: for every minute of interview time, you need at least one minute of preparation and/or cleanup time. So if your interview is twenty minutes long, you'll need to schedule at least an additional twenty minutes of your time. Probably a few beforehand to get everything set up and several minutes afterward to make sense of your notes and clean up. Be sure to budget this time as you're planning your interviews. I've seen too many people schedule interviews back to back to back and end up confused and exhausted. All the interviews seem to run together and they can't remember what anyone said.

You need time in between your interviews to gather and refine your notes, jot down anything you haven't had time to capture during the interview, and make sure you have all the notes you need to help you remember important information later. When you don't do this, you risk missing or losing important insights that could help shape your product. It can literally be the difference between a good product and a great one.

SETTING UP THE INTERVIEW

Have everything set up before your interviewee arrives. You want them to feel you have your act together, and nothing ruins that impression like someone scrambling to find their pen and notepad, or struggling to get the audio recorder to work.

Use whatever notepad or paper you're comfortable with. My team uses everything from legal pads to Moleskine notebooks. It doesn't really matter. What matters is that you can capture as much as possible with minimal fuss. Use what works for you. I recommend using paper for a few reasons:

1. It's less noisy than clacking away on your laptop's keyboard.
2. It allows you to be more freeform, which leads to more freeform conversations.
3. A laptop screen creates a little wall between you and the invitee, and you don't want a wall there. You want the communication to be free and open.
4. Pen and paper don't require batteries! One less thing to worry about charging.

Whether you're interviewing someone remotely or in person, always record the interview so you can refer back to it in later exercises. Always test your equipment beforehand and have a backup ready if possible. Make sure your phone or pocket audio recorder is fully charged and take extra chargers and batteries just in case.

Before the interviewee arrives, write down their name, the date, and the number interview they are. For your first interview, write the number 1, write 2 for the second, and so on. This will serve as an ID number later in the process.

Also, go ahead and start the audio recording and say these same things for the recording. That way when you go back to listen to the recording, you can tell if you have the right audio at the very beginning. This sounds tedious, but do it anyway. Many years ago, I wasted about four hours on a project just trying to find the right audio file.

It's good if you can have someone assist you by taking notes in the interviews. That way you can stay focused on listening to the interviewee and asking good questions. If you do have an assistant, have them sit behind you and to the side so they are visible but not distracting.

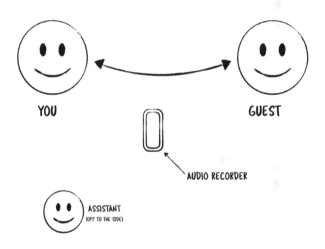

Introduce them to the interviewee with something like:

"This is my colleague, Chris. He'll be taking notes so I

can pay better attention to you and we can have a good conversation."

This last bit about "a good conversation" is important. You're setting the tone that you're interested in having a conversation, not an interrogation. The interviewee should never feel like they're on the witness stand. You get the best, most candid and truthful, answers when the interviewee is relaxed and feels like you're genuinely interested in them.

Make sure your recording device is on the table between you and the interviewee and say:

"With your permission I'd like to record the conversation so we can refer to it later when we're compiling our notes. Just in case Chris over here misses something. The recording will be completely confidential and we'll destroy it after we've compiled our notes."

Now the interviewee knows the conversation is being recorded and you've given them comfort the recording will be safe.

Note that some people might object to being recorded. If this happens, just say "Okay," put the recording device away in a bag or out of sight, and proceed without the recording. Also write down that no recording was made for them on your notes so you're not pulling your hair out later when you can't find the audio file.

With all that out of the way you're ready to begin!

CONDUCTING THE INTERVIEW

Remember to avoid introducing your own bias as much as possible. You want to learn about them and their world and what they are trying to do. You're not trying to see if they like your idea. You are trying to document who you are interviewing, what situation they're in, and what they're trying to accomplish. For example: a realtor in a large firm who is trying to grow their book of business, a working mother who is trying to handle all her responsibilities, an athlete who wants to track their nutrition and exercise goals. You get the idea.

> Pro Tip: Take a quick look at the Empathy Map to get an idea of the things you want to understand more about. What do they see, say, hear, and do? We'll come back to the Empathy Map later on, but having it in mind as you're doing the interviews will help you get the most out of each interview.

You want to ask open-ended questions that get them telling stories. Here are some great ones to get started.

- So I understand you are [a realtor/an athlete/in sales]. What's that like?
- Can you tell me about your typical day?
- What's the most frustrating thing about being [a realtor/an athlete/in sales]?
- What do you wish you had more of?

You get the idea. Ask broad, open-ended questions to get started and get more detailed from there. Avoid any question that can be answered either yes or no.

The goal is to get them telling stories about real things that happened to them because that's where the gold is. Gold? Yes, their needs, wants, and fears are the gold you're after. You want them to talk about what they struggle with, what they need or want more or less of, and what scares them. This is where you'll find the truth about how to build a product that will deliver real value to them.

Good interview questions can be divided into three basic categories: stage setters, explorers, and refiners.

Examples of stage setters:

- I understand you are a _____.
- I'd like to learn about _____.

Examples of explorers:

- Tell me about your typical day.
- What frustrates you about [a task]?
- What have you tried?
- What do you think other people do?

Examples of refiners:

- Interesting. Can you tell me more about that?
- Help me understand what you mean.
- What do you mean by _____?

These questions might seem like they don't lead any-where. Just trust me on this. When you get someone telling a story about how Gary in accounting always messes up the spreadsheet and it costs them two hours of every week just to clean up the mess, you've struck gold.

To download our interview question cheat sheet, visit Loopsbook.com/resources.

POST-INTERVIEW CLEANUP

Now that the interview is over, do a few quick tasks to wrap up and make all the notes easier to find later. You should already have the name, date, and ID on the paper notes. If you have time, it might be a good idea to take photos of the paper notes. That's a quick and dirty backup if something happens to the paper ones.

When naming your audio files, do something like:

ProjectName_SubjectName_YYYYMMDD_HH:MM.

Your actual file name might look something like this:

TacoAppResearch_SusanParsons_20190529_13:30.mp3

Keep the same naming convention for all your recordings. This makes it super easy to find files in the future, and it also keeps them all nicely sorted on your computer. Again, it might seem tedious, but it will save you time. You'll thank me later.

After your interviews, you'll want to transcribe all your notes from the notepad to an Empathy Map for this person. Do them for one interviewee at a time and get everything from the interview into a section on the Empathy Map that makes the most sense to you.

Start with the name, date, and ID number, then add information about the basic demographics in section 1, write the task(s) they are trying to accomplish in section 2, then move on to the meat of the interview notes. You're separating the things you heard into the main sections: See, Say, Do, Hear, Pains, and Gains. It's not an exact science, and sometimes a thought will seem like it could belong in two sections. Just pick one that makes the most sense, and maybe draw an arrow to the other one just so you remember later.

Wait. Why didn't we just take notes on the Empathy Map in the first place?

Glad you asked. Using the Empathy Map to capture the notes generally slows you down and drops the quality of your notes because you're too busy thinking about which section to write the notes in! Capturing notes is one thing. Making sense of them is another.

When you complete each Empathy Map, take a photo of it, then file it with the interview notes for later reference. Wash, rinse, and repeat until you have completed Empathy Maps for each person you interviewed.

Now you're ready for the next step. Take a break. You've earned a drink.

AFFINITY MAPPING

Let's say you talk to fifty people during your first round of interviews. By now, you should have a clearer picture of your demographics, and the psychographics should be coming into focus. The next step is to use the Empathy Maps you created for each actor you interviewed to assemble an Affinity Map, which will help define the role that has your problem.

INTERVIEW BEST PRACTICES

- An app like Calendly can help you easily schedule interviews and ask basic questions of people beforehand.

- If you're interviewing people remotely, you can use Zoom, which has both free and paid plans, for recording audio and video interviews.

- If you're meeting up with someone in person, offer to buy them a cup of coffee or tea. For longer interviews, offer to take them out to lunch. When you're interviewing someone remotely, offer to send them a Starbucks or Amazon gift card after they participate. Don't overthink it, just tailor the value of the incentive to the amount of time you're asking of someone.

- Mentally prepare. Get in the right mindset before the interview. Focus on removing your bias and just listening to learn about the human in front of you.

- Allow ample time. Plan time before and after the interview to prep and wrap up.

- Bring an audio recorder. Your phone will be fine, but a dedicated recorder will deliver better quality audio. It also looks more professional and is not as distracting.

- Keep it casual and conversational. This is not an interrogation. Let the conversation flow like you're talking to a friend.

- Don't try to find specific answers. Instead, try to get them telling a story about the problem they have.

- Don't focus too hard on one thing. It's okay if you don't get the exact answer you're looking for. You're going to talk to lots of people, and if that answer is important, you'll hear it from someone else.

- Silence can be your friend. Don't feel like you have to fill every moment with conversation. Sometimes asking a question and just sitting there while the interviewee thinks for a moment gives them time to remember a story to tell.

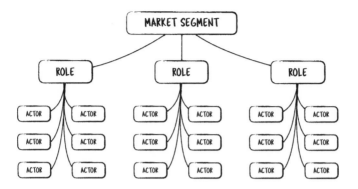

Affinity Mapping is an exercise that helps you and your team take the data you've compiled and find patterns and themes about the people you talked to. This will help shape the product you build specifically to their needs, wants, and fears.

You'll create Affinity Maps after each round of interviews to further refine your target market and how they think about their problems. As you go, you'll gain more confidence that you're solving the right problem for them. It's good to involve your team in this process so everyone can see how your understanding of the market evolves. That will help everyone stay aligned as we go through the rest of the process.

To get started, you're going to need several stacks of differently colored sticky notes. Ideally, you'll have seven or eight colors. Bigger stickies are generally better (depending on your handwriting). You'll also need a large wall or whiteboard. You need plenty of space to spread out. I recommend at least an eight-by-four-foot work area. You could also use a table, but a wall works best. It could be in your office or house or a rented meeting room. Location doesn't really matter so long as it's quiet, private, and you have enough space.

Step 1: Gather all the materials: different color sticky notes, markers or a pen, and a large wall.

Step 2: Gather your Empathy Maps and start writing the thoughts from each section on sticky notes. One thought per sticky. Make sure you write the number from the Empathy Map you're working on in the corner of each sticky. That will help you trace things back later on. It helps to use the same color sticky for all the thoughts from one section. For example, all notes from See might be blue and all thoughts from Do might be green. You choose which color to use for what, just stay consistent across all Empathy Maps, forever. Don't use blue for See on one Empathy Map and for Do on another. We use blue for See, yellow for Say, green for Do, and pink for Hear. You can use whatever colors you like.

Don't try to organize anything or group the stickies at this point. Resist the temptation to put colors together or similar words together. In fact, it helps to have one person writing on the sticky notes and another person putting them up on the wall. The only thing you're trying to do now is get everything off of the Empathy Maps and up on the wall.

Also, this is a silent process. Don't discuss or even think too hard about the notes you're putting on the wall. You can listen to music, but don't talk about what you're doing. You'll see why soon.

Once all the stickies are up on the wall, take a ten- to fifteen-minute break. Don't talk about notes or anything you've done so far. Leave the room and let your brain have a little rest. Things are about to get interesting.

GROUPING

When you come back, start looking for patterns or commonalities that are emerging. When you see notes that are similar (not by color or ID), group them together on the wall. Maybe you see the phrase "frustrating to use" appearing multiple times, or the phrase "I need more time in my day" keeps popping up. Group these thoughts together. It doesn't have to be the exact same wording or come from the same place on the Empathy Map. In other words, ignore the sticky note colors at this point and focus on grouping similar thoughts.

Sometimes you and your team might not be able to decide where a sticky note should go. If possible, don't discuss it—just move the notes around to where people generally agree. If you absolutely can't agree on where it goes, just make a copy of the note and put one in each location. Write "Copy" on each note so you know to look for the other.

Once you group the similar thoughts together, take out a clean Empathy Map and start to put the things from the wall back on the Empathy Map in a way that makes sense to you. This will become the aggregate Empathy Map for this group of people and will be the starting point for the Role Empathy Map. You'll do an Affinity Map exercise for each group of people you interview and use that to update your Role Empathy Maps.

Using our real estate example from earlier, you might see a role emerge that doesn't like to use spreadsheets (problem) for lead follow-up (task) because leads don't get called back quickly enough (pain point). The gain might be that they'll convert more leads and make more money with quicker follow-up.

Another role might be realtors who don't like to use spreadsheets (problem) for managing their past clients (task) because it's not detailed enough (pain point). The gain might be creating more repeat business because the realtor checked in more often with old clients.

A third role could be realtors who don't like to use spreadsheets (problem) to track their commission totals (task) because they aren't secure enough for financial data (pain point). The gain is a greater sense of security when their payment data isn't at risk.

Focus on the tasks, pains, and gains as you create your Role Empathy Maps. Depending on how many Empathy Maps you have, this process could take one hour or several hours. Don't stress about how long it takes. It's very important to finish this exercise for every round of interviews you do to guide you during every step of the process from now on.

THE SECOND ROUND OF INTERVIEWS

The goal of the first round of interviews was to start defining a subset of the people who share a common problem. The Affinity Mapping process helps identify common threads in that subset of people. For the second round of interviews, you want to choose at least one criterion to refine your target audience (e.g., age, experience, location) so you can narrow your focus. It's good if you can choose two criteria (e.g., age *and* location), but you don't want to refine by more than two criteria because you risk getting too narrow of an audience and going down a rabbit hole.

For example, you might come away from the first round

knowing you need to target real estate brokers who live in Atlanta (criteria #1) and sell houses that cost more than $800,000 (criteria #2). Don't talk to anyone outside the group for the second round. Use the recruitment strategies we discussed to find people who match your criteria.

The aim of this round of interviews is the same as before: further refine the problem you're trying to solve and who you're solving it for. Be aware of your biases, remain open-minded, and go where the data shows you to go. Keep the Empathy Map in mind as you interview people and focus on getting them to tell stories. At the end of every interview, ask the interviewee if you can follow up later when it's time to test your solution. If they say yes, save their contact information and promise to follow up later.

I can't tell you how many people you'll need to talk to during this round of interviews or the rounds that follow. There's no way to predict how many people you'll have to talk to and how many Roles will emerge from your research. It all depends on what kind of problem you're exploring and the people you're interviewing. You might need twenty interviews; you might need two hundred. You'll know that it's okay to stop when you start to feel confident about how well you understand the problem. Ideally, you'll have it down to a very specific type of person with a very specific problem. We call this a Problem Statement, and creating a great Problem Statement is the goal of all this research. Something like this:

Realtors under the age of 36 who work in large firms, in urban areas with over 1 million residents, and sell single-family homes worth over $800,000 struggle with spreadsheets and legacy software tools for contact management. They spend too much time searching and sorting contacts to find the right match for a potential sale. They want a way to quickly find contacts while on their phones, and be able to call, text, or email that contact information about a property with just a few taps. Having such a tool would save them at least an hour per day, eliminate frustration, and lead to more business.

See how precise that is? With that Problem Statement, you know exactly who you're targeting, what their problem is, what their pains are, and what they stand to gain.

OVERCOMING THE CURVE OF DESPAIR

The question I often get from people at this point is, "When do I know that I'm ready to move on from the interviews?" The answer comes back to confidence. With each round of interviews, you'll gain more knowledge and confidence. Think of it like a teeter-totter. You're standing near the side that's in the air, and every time you talk to someone, you add weight to that side. When you add enough to make that teeter-totter tip, you're ready to move to the last part of the research phase: creating a Value Proposition Canvas.

Check out the confidence curve graphic (also affectionately called the Curve of Despair) to see how confidence dips and then builds as you move through the research phase:

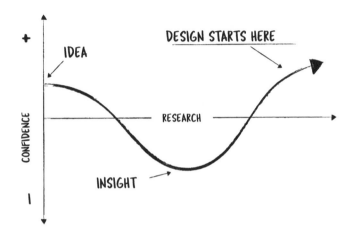

Nobody can tell you when that level of confidence will come. It really is a gut feeling.

LET'S TALK ABOUT MONEY

That said, there is a measure of confidence that people sometimes overlook: money. If the people you talk to ask to give you money to solve the problem, you should have

ROOT CAUSE ANALYSIS

When you're interviewing someone and you want to understand what's truly causing them pain, there's a great technique I recommend called *root cause analysis*, also known as the "five whys."

It basically boils down to being like an annoying three-year-old who never stops asking, "Why?" To show the power of root cause analysis, here's a story about the Washington Monument.

About a decade ago, the people responsible for maintaining the Washington Monument came to the General Service Administration with a problem: the monument was deteriorating at an accelerated pace. The worst part was no one could explain why it was crumbling faster than all the other granite monuments in Washington, DC.

Turns out, the harsh detergent that was being used to keep the monument clean was contributing to its deterioration. Why was that detergent only being used on the Washington Monument? Well, because birds were pooping on the monument at a ridiculously high rate.

Why were the birds pooping on the monument so much? Turns out, the monument attracted tons of birds because it was covered in bugs they wanted to eat. Why were these bugs all over the Washington Monument and not every other monument in the city?

The bugs were there because of the lights that illuminated the monument at night. The bugs brought the birds, who pooped on the monument and necessitated the use of a harsh detergent that was causing the monument to crumble. Change the lights and the bugs won't come, the birds will go away, the monument won't get pooped on, the harsh detergent won't be necessary to keep it clean, and the monument's deterioration will slow.

When you talk to people and they say their problem is the detergent, don't assume that's the root of their problem. Keep asking, "Why?" until you get to the lights.

a level of confidence that you're onto the right solution for the right people. You might hear this comment from interview subjects who say they'd pay you to solve their problem. You might also be able to raise venture capital money based just on an idea you pitch. Of the two, hearing it from the people you interview is the best measure since they represent your potential customers.

The topic of money brings up an important rule for interviews: don't ask people how much they would pay for a solution to their problem. At this point, most won't have the context or understand the value of a solution fully enough to give you an accurate answer.

However, you can ask questions that might lead them to throw out a price, or at least a signal of value:

What would it mean to you if this problem was solved?

How much time and/or money would you save if this problem was solved?

These questions can help the customer start to see the value in a solution to their problem and potentially lead them to say they'd pay money to whoever could solve it. At the least, you'll get a sense for how much they might value a solution. Sometimes they will respond with something like, "Oh wow, I'd give you $1,000 to solve that," or "This problem costs my company $2 million a year," or even, "That would save the business dozens of hours each week." Those types of responses indicate real value. Make sure to write this stuff down because they will come in very handy in the next phase of work, creating your Value Proposition Canvas.

VALUE PROPOSITION CANVAS

Once you've developed a high level of confidence that you understand the problem you're trying to solve and who you're trying to solve it for, the next step is to start creating a Value Proposition Canvas for each role you've identified.

The Value Proposition Canvas is a tool developed by the team at Strategyzer to help executives and product teams define and discuss what really matters to people.

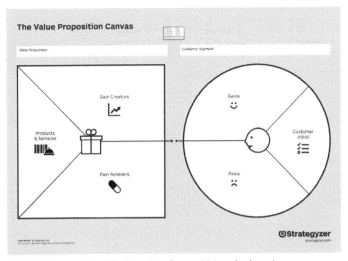

To download a copy of the Value Proposition Canvas, visit Loopsbook.com/resources.

Take out those Role Empathy Maps. We're going to need them to fill in the right half of your Value Proposition Canvas. As you probably remember, we focused on tasks, pains, and gains during Affinity Mapping because that info is needed here. On the right side, fill in the task each role is trying to accomplish as well as the *pains* and *gains* associated with each one.

On the left side is where you'll start to define the Value Proposition your product needs to provide. Remember, the Value Proposition is what your customers are *really* buying from you. It's also what makes your product unique and distinguishes you from the competition.

For example, Amazon isn't *really* selling products. Most

of what you find on Amazon is available in several other places at comparable prices. Amazon *actually* sells speed, convenience, and free Prime shipping.

FEATURES AND BENEFITS

It's important to think about both features and benefits when you're creating a Value Proposition. What's the difference? Features are generally quantifiable or tangible. Usually, they relate to a specification of a product or service. Benefits are generally outcomes that a product or service can make possible. Features are measurable. Benefits are more emotional.

Another way to think about the difference between features and benefits is to look at the way Android and iPhone devices are marketed and advertised. In a typical Android phone commercial, they talk about the gigabytes of storage and the multimegapixel cameras on the front and back of the phone. The phone has a seven-inch screen that's made from unbreakable glass. All of the "important specifications" are touted in the commercial. They do a wonderful job. It's a well-produced, beautiful, compelling commercial, and it tells me exactly what I need to know about the features of the device.

Now think about an iPhone commercial. It's essentially the same device, right? It has two cameras. It has a similar-sized screen and similar specs on processing power and memory. Yet iPhone commercials are profoundly different. Apple advertises the iPhone by showing you a video of something personal. Maybe a family reunion, a student graduating, or someone proposing to their significant other. They use video and content that connects with your emotions but is still related to the way you use your iPhone. Once the tears are rolling, they end with "Created on iPhone."

You don't care how many megapixels the camera has, or how big the phone is. You care about how the phone empowers you to capture moments that matter. Android is talking about the features; Apple is showing you the benefits. Big difference.

Analytical people will be moved to purchase by features that impress them or suit their specific needs. People make decisions based more on emotions look to make purchases when they know the benefits they'll get. That said, humans are weird and don't fit neatly into "analytical" and "emotional" boxes. People buy things based on different stimuli and information, but they also make decisions based on different needs at different times. Someone who leans more analytical will make a decision based on emotion in certain conditions, and the opposite is also true. When you build your Value Proposition, you need to consider and include both features and benefits.

To give you an example, let's return to the realtor who doesn't like to use spreadsheets for managing their clients because it's not detailed enough. The gain they wanted was more repeat business because the realtor checked in more often with past clients. In this case, a Pain Reliever might be software that automatically records and tracks up to one hundred stats about a client. The one hundred stats is a quantifiable *feature*. The *benefit* for the realtor is not having to remember all those details anymore.

An example of a Gain Creator might be customized follow-up templates that help clients feel remembered and special on their anniversary or birthday. The templates are a *feature*. The improved relationship with the client is a *benefit*.

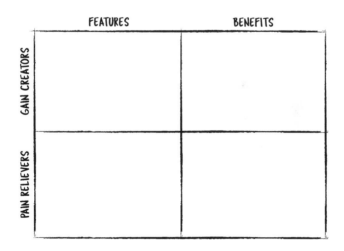

To download a copy of the Features & Benefits Canvas, visit Loopsbook.com/resources.

At this point, you should have the right side of your Value Proposition Canvas filled out with the tasks people are trying to accomplish and the pains and gains related to those tasks. Set the canvas aside for now. It's time to get to work coming up with something that helps them accomplish the task while relieving pains and creating gains. We'll tackle that in the next chapter.

I know the research process seems like a lot of work, but ultimately, you'll understand your market better than anybody else. The better you understand your market, the bigger your advantage over the competition. The more work you do now, the better chance you have of creating a solution that's not just useful and usable, but also desirable.

HOW IT ALL FITS TOGETHER

Ultimately, your Empathy Maps help you define your Value Proposition, which helps define your business model. The *pains* and *gains* from your Empathy Map are used to fill in the *pains* and *gains* in your Value Proposition. Then your Value Proposition is used in your Business Model Canvas (another Strategyzer tool). Your Empathy Maps define your Customer Segments, and those also go into your Business Model Canvas.

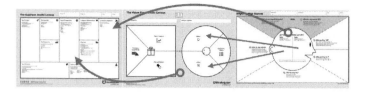

For a closer look at how everything fits together, visit Loopsbook.com/resources.

Now you see why defining these things early on is a huge benefit to defining your business model, and why investing the time now will pay off later when you're figuring out how to build a business around your product.

MAILCHIMP KNOWS ITS CUSTOMERS

Mailchimp exemplifies the value of research in the early stages of human-centered design. The cool thing is that you have a leg up over the guys who started Mailchimp since you get to follow a defined process that was mostly done by trial and error and gut feelings until now.

Mailchimp is fantastic at understanding their customers. When they started out, they wanted to know what pains and gains their customers had around reliably sending good-looking bulk emails. If you're curious what a sample Value Proposition canvas might look like for Mailchimp, here's one I put together for them:

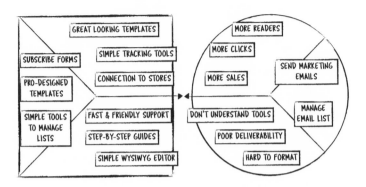

Mailchimp wasn't the first bulk email company, but their success is unmatched now because they designed a solution that solved a problem many people had in a way those people connected to. In doing so, they built a product people love and engendered loyalty amongst their customers.

To this day, Mailchimp still listens closely to their customers. The result is that Mailchimp continues to grow exponentially every year and likely will for the foreseeable future.

HOW DO WE DO IT?

Did you know Facebook updates their platform multiple times per day? It might be a handful of updates or hundreds, but they're always testing new ideas. The Facebook team goes through a process like you just did—identifying a problem and validating it through research—and then they test these solutions with small groups of users.

Maybe Facebook wants to increase the number of soccer fans who create groups for other soccer fans, so they move the "Create a Group" button to a more visible place on the top navigation, then release the update to 10,000 soccer fans to see what happens. If their solution is validated through testing, Facebook pushes that update live across the site to more and more people in a series of small updates.

In this phase of human-centered business design, you're going to do what Facebook does: develop a solution and test it. You've validated a problem, and now it's time to design a solution, prototype it, and put it in the hands of customers who can give feedback.

Interestingly, Facebook employees must write a defense of their idea before it can be deployed and tested. If their peers decide the idea has merit, it gets developed.

You don't have to write a defense of your solution, but you will engage in a collaborative process that involves putting every idea your team has under the microscope. Only the best ones get prototyped and sent out into the world for testing. The ones that survive and get refined by user feedback might just make it to the final round of this process.

For now, let's answer the question: How do we do it?

Chapter Three

STEP TWO: PROTOTYPING

"Unless you have fixed costs, you don't need any capital to create a prototype. Ideally, your co-founders, with sweat equity, can create the product themselves."

BRIAN CHESKY, CO-FOUNDER, AIRBNB

After Mailchimp validated the problem their customers had—no reliable way of sending good-looking emails—and validated there were enough people with this problem to try making a product, it was time to start prototyping. This is the second step of the human-centered business design process, and it begins with asking yourself:

How might we _____?

For Mailchimp, they started by asking themselves, "How might we create great-looking emails that show up the right way in all the popular email apps?" Before the first email ever got sent, Mailchimp needed to lock down that part of the equation. To get there, they built and tested hundreds of email templates before finding ones that consistently looked great on Gmail, Outlook, Yahoo, and all the desktop email apps that were popular at the time. They used these templates to send email on behalf of their clients. Clients were happy and asked them to send more email.

As the service became more popular, they realized there was no way to manually send all the emails for all the clients. There just wasn't enough time in the day. So they went to the next step: self-service.

The same process unfolded when Mailchimp decided to design a tool for clients to send bulk emails using the templates they had created. They considered several options: maybe a piece of desktop software, a web-based platform, or a plugin for all the email apps. Ultimately, Mailchimp created a web-based platform that's now used by millions of people around the world.

They focused on solving the customer's problem, not validating what they wanted to build. That's what led to their success.

Mailchimp used *wireframes*, *prototypes*, and *user journeys* to understand their users' needs and create something that addressed them. We'll walk through these processes in the upcoming pages of the book. They continue to build little experiments and prototypes and test them with people to this day. It's how they continue to improve the product some eighteen years later.

DESIGNING SOLUTIONS

Keep in mind that the prototyping phase, which includes wireframing, user journeys, and lots of other activities, is about *solution design* and not *product design*. We'll get to product design later in the process, but right now, we're focused on designing something to solve a customer's problem. It's too early to start thinking about products. You have to remain fluid and open to how people in your target market respond to your ideas. To start designing products at this stage would lock you into a way of thinking or going down a path that would be counterproductive to the process and potentially waste lots of time and money.

In this chapter, you'll learn to build cheap experiments and prototypes you can test with your target market. You'll learn how to tell when something works and when it doesn't. If it works, awesome. If not, you didn't waste your time and money building something nobody wants.

A NOTE ON CREATING NEW MARKETS

In some cases, you might be creating a market where one didn't exist before. For example, there was no mass-demand for a service like Uber before Uber. There was certainly a demand for transportation, but not in the way Uber does it today. People just took taxis, public transit, or drove their own cars. There was an extremely small (almost nonexistent) market for on-demand car services before Uber, but it was really only used by the wealthy. When Uber started, they didn't look at the market for on-demand car services because that was a very small percentage of people. They broadened their scope to people who need to get somewhere, and that was a very big market.

By zooming out to a macro level, Travis Kalanick and Garrett Camp saw a problem most of the public didn't even realize it had. I remember Travis telling me the story of he and Garrett sitting on a curb in Paris amazed he couldn't call a taxi with his smartphone. It was a "Why doesn't this exist?" moment. Remember the question from Chapter 1: "Is there a version of the future where this doesn't exist?" They asked that question, and they were right. People weren't asking for on-demand car service, but they eventually saw the value when it was offered to them.

There's always a risk with trying to create your own market. Not only must you educate customers on who you are and the value of your solution—you have to first educate them on a problem they don't know they have! Early on, people didn't understand Uber's value or the problem Uber solved until early adopters started using the service and raving about it.

It's easier if you're trying to tap into an existing market, but creating your own market is not impossible, just riskier. To be successful will cost more time, effort, and money, and require a thorough understanding of what is possible and what the market needs.

As we go through the prototyping phase, keep in mind that you're looking to prove a few things. Your solution must:

- Solve the problem you identified in Step 1.
- Solve it in a way that creates value for the customer you identified in Step 1.
- Solve it in a way that generates profit for the business.

About that last point, profit: this inevitably leads to a discussion of price. If people indicated during interviews that they'd pay for a solution, you can have some confidence that other customers with that problem would be willing to pay too. That said, you won't know exactly how much customers will pay until you go back to them with a potential solution and they can see the value in your product. Also, remember that value is mostly a matter of perception. Remember *Exchange Theory* from Chapter 1? Pricing is a tricky art and it's too early to get fixated on price now, especially since you haven't made a product yet, so you have no idea how much it costs to make! Don't worry, we'll come back to pricing in a little while.

TOOLS FOR PROTOTYPING

- A whiteboard
- Dry-erase markers
- Sticky notes
- Sharpies
- Pencils and pens
- Notepads

The whiteboard is indispensable during this phase because it's a fast, easy, low-fidelity, low-friction way to facilitate conversation and decision-making. Get one as big as you can fit on your wall or go get whiteboard paint and paint the whole wall. If that's not an option, rent a room at your local coworking spot. No matter how you choose to get a whiteboard for this process, it will be worth the investment.

Pro Tip: don't put the Sharpies and the dry-erase markers in the same box! Speaking from experience, someone will inevitably grab a Sharpie and write on your whiteboard.

Perhaps most importantly, you need your Value Proposition Canvases. As you're working through these exercises, you have to keep the Value Propositions in front of you. Print the canvases out and stick them somewhere that they'll be the center of attention for your team.

IDEA GENERATION

The first step to solving any problem is coming up with some ideas on how you might do it. There's more than one way to skin a cat, as they say, but some ways are better than others. What you'll do next is gather your team and spend some time coming up with a few ways to solve a problem for your target market. It's one of the more fun parts of the process, so gather some supplies and let's get started. You're going to need:

- A quiet room with room for you and your team to move around.
- A large whiteboard or wall (bigger is better)
- Pens and sticky notes
- Resist the urge to rush through this part of the process. It's critically important to take your time and make smart decisions. This stage will take at least three days on the calendar, but only a handful of hours of actual work. You'll see why soon.

DIVERGENT THINKING

To begin building a list of potential solutions, return to that core question:

How might we _____?

Bring your team together to brainstorm answers to that

question. This is using *divergent thinking*, which means giving room for spontaneous, free-flowing thoughts that can be as random, off-the-wall, or crazy as you want so long as they solve the problem.

You'll need the Sharpies, whiteboard, and sticky notes. Every time someone throws out an idea, no matter how wild it is, write it down on a sticky note and put it on the whiteboard. Don't worry about organization right now. Just be sure to write the idea legibly enough that you can read it, and include enough detail so you'll remember what it was and understand it later.

You might start a little slow, but then the ideas will start to flow. Just keep going and don't try to comment or discuss the merits of any idea at this point. Just get them on the wall. After a while, ideas will start to come slower and slower. Don't be concerned. This is normal. Allow the uncomfortable silence to linger. Let people sit and think for a bit rather than urging them to come up with more ideas. If people need to get up and walk around, that's cool. Some of us need to fidget in order to think. Let that uncomfortable silence linger as long as needed. More ideas will come—don't quit when you think they're starting to run out! Take a break if you need to, but don't quit. Not yet. You'll know when everyone is truly out of ideas because you'll all be physically and mentally exhausted, like you just ran a mile. That's when it's time to call it a day.

If nobody else needs the wall space, you can leave the sticky notes up. If you can't leave them up, take several photos of the wall, making sure you capture everything. Either way, be sure someone on the team puts all the ideas into a spreadsheet, one idea per line.

THE SOAK

The next step is what I call "the Soak." When you cook a nice marinara, you put all the ingredients in a pot and you let them simmer for a while. You'll do the same here with all the ideas you and your team threw up on the wall.

It's best to spend at least two days away from the whiteboard and give your slow-thinking brain time to work through all the new ideas. Remember, your slow-thinking brain thinks about things from more angles and goes through things more thoroughly, but it does so at a level you're not consciously aware of. Your slow-thinking brain needs time to soak.

When you come back to your ideas, there's likely one or two that have been bubbling up in your mind during the Soak. You almost certainly have a favorite. You might not be sure why, but you can't stop thinking about it. It pops into your mind at random times, like when you're stuck in traffic or out for a run. This is your subconscious, slow-thinking brain, telling you that this idea might be worthwhile. That's not to say this idea is the absolute right answer, just that it's worth exploring more. You might be drawn to multiple ideas—and your team will have their own favorites. That's okay. Trust your instincts and come back to the whiteboard ready to discuss your favorite idea and why you like it so much.

CONVERGENT THINKING

When you get back with your team after the Soak, it's time to dive into *convergent thinking*, which means distilling all the ideas you have into one (or more) cohesive solutions. Bring back the same team that went through the divergent thinking exercise and look at all your ideas for possible solutions again. If your sticky notes are still up on the wall, give each person a different color marker and have them put a check next to the ideas they like. Different colored sticky dots like you had in elementary school are also good for this.

Don't take any ideas down at this point, but tally the check marks or colored dots from the sticky notes on the spreadsheet. As you go through convergent thinking, some ideas might merge with others. That's cool. The goal is to narrow your batch of ideas down to the three to five options that make the most sense. From there, work with your team to rank the ideas based on viability, which means answering two questions:

- Will the customer be able to see the value in this solution?
- If so, is your team capable of building a prototype of it?

This is when it's vital to have the Value Proposition canvas handy. Keep the focus on solving the customer's problem. Even if an idea is revolutionary, if it doesn't offer the value you defined in the research phase, it's not worth pursuing. Once you narrow the list down to a few choices the team feels good about, it's time to start wireframing and prototyping.

ADAPTLY PLAYED IT SMART

To see how the research process flows into this prototyping phase, let's look at the story of a startup who did things a bit unconventionally. Adaptly was started by Garrett Ullom and Nikhil Sethi, who saw what they thought was a need in social media marketing optimization for big brands. Their first step was to talk with colleagues and others in that space to make sure they were heading down the right path. To use a term I like, they wanted to ensure they were *directionally accurate*.

By talking with people who worked in social media marketing, Garrett and Nikhil's idea became a hunch, and the problem they wanted to solve came into sharper focus. Then things got interesting.

Garrett and Nikhil now knew they had a problem that might be worth solving. What they didn't know was the size of the market, how potent the demand was, or how acutely the target audience felt this pain. They decided to get answers—*before writing a single line of code.*

They put up a landing page that made the service look functional and communicated a Value Proposition along the lines of: "Get more bang for your advertising buck." The landing page just asked for an email address to get access to the platform. Then they marketed that landing page to the people they thought might have this problem using Google and other ad platforms. As traffic came in, they fine-tuned the message based on conversion rates, that is, looking at how many people put in their email address versus those who simply visited the site. Ultimately, Garrett and Nikhil found a Value Proposition that was a bulls-eye for their market.

At this point, they still hadn't written code. Next, they created a form for customers to submit information about the campaigns they were running, where they were running them, and what they were being charged. Garrett and Nikhil took that data and manually did all the work in the background using some fancy spreadsheets. Then they generated reports for customers with suggestions for how they could optimize their ad spend. Customers loved it and were happy to pay for a solution. They didn't know that it was all done manually, and it's unlikely they would have cared. All customers cared about was having their problem solved.

The prototype Garrett and Nikhil developed solved that problem, proved that people would pay for a solution, and validated their hunch. In doing the work manually at first, these guys saw the repeated processes for which they could write code and generated the revenue needed to write that code and develop the software.

They set themselves up for success by building a product the right way from the start. When I say success, I mean *big-time* success. In December 2018, Adaptly was acquired by Accenture Interactive. Not bad for two guys who started with just an idea!

The story of Adaptly exemplifies the way you should operate during this process: run things as lean as possible to make sure that you're going down the right path.

Garrett and Nikhil didn't know exactly what their solution would look like when they started out. That's why they designed a low-tech, low-cost prototype that they could test with customers and then implement changes based on their feedback. Everything from their landing page and the Value Proposition to the spreadsheets they used and the reports they generated went through several iterations as they tested their solutions.

By going through the three-step brainstorm process, they came up with solutions to test. Garrett and Nikhil developed a lean, low-cost prototype to test those solutions.

CREATING SOMETHING YOU CAN TEST

By now, you should have one to three potential solutions you'd like to test with your target market to see what works. The next few exercises are important parts of the process, and to do them well will take some practice and further reading.

Rather than go through each one in painful detail, I've opted to give you an overview and references to other great books and materials which will give you the nitty-gritty on each process or exercise.

The big picture is you want to go from the concept you wrote on those stickies to something you can show people and get valuable feedback on. This process of prototyping and testing is a never-ending loop that you will use to continuously improve your products based on real human needs.

We start with a *User Journey Map*, then create *Wireframes* of some basic workflows and interfaces, then create *Paper Prototypes*, before finally moving on to *Digital Prototypes*. You'll increase the fidelity, or accuracy in visual appearance and functionality on each Loop, until eventually you'll have a prototype that looks and feels like a finished product (even though it won't be).

Don't worry, you'll be able to create something people can actually use and pay for pretty early in the process. This overview is meant to show you what happens in each Loop. You'll probably ship something people can use after a few Loops, but continue to use the Loop process to refine and improve the product as you grow and build the business, much like Mailchimp has been doing for years.

USER JOURNEYS

The starting Loop of your larger prototyping and testing Loop is to map out the *User Journey*. A User Journey is what it sounds like: the journey a user goes on when trying to accomplish a task. For example, you might think it's pretty easy to open your phone and post something on social media. True, but when we break down all the steps it actually takes, it begins to shed light on how we might improve the process. And remember, different platforms do things slightly differently. The process to post to Instagram is different than posting to Snapchat, even though you're really just posting a photo.

User Journey Maps (some people might call them storyboards) will help you and your team understand and document the steps someone needs to take to successfully accomplish a task. To break it down, you need to think about *sequencing*, breaking the process into small steps so you can better understand each one.

Let's pretend we're making a taco delivery app, because everyone loves tacos. We'll start by listing each major step someone has to do to successfully complete the task. For example:

1. Open the app
2. Choose a taco
3. Choose a delivery address
4. Pay for the taco
5. Complete the order

Simple enough. But there are other things involved if you look a little closer.

1. Get your phone out of your pocket/purse/bag
2. Unlock the phone
3. Locate the app icon
4. Open the app
5. Wait for the app to load
6. Go to the taco menu
7. Choose a taco

8. Choose ingredients (chicken, beans, rice, etc.)
9. Add to cart
10. Wait for visual or audio indication the taco was added to the cart
11. Repeat if you want more tacos
12. View cart
13. And so on...

You get the idea. Creating a User Journey needs to be pretty detailed so you can find opportunities to create value for the user.

Now that you understand the process, draw a box on the whiteboard or use a sticky note to describe each step of the User Journey. This will help you see how to design your product's workflow to make sure it does what the user needs (useful), does it in a way that's easy to use (usable), and find ways to simplify the process and make it fun (desirable).

In the end, you want your User Journey Map to show a view of how your product supports the user getting to a successful outcome.

A lot of great material has been written about creating great user journeys, so I suggest you check out *Mapping Experiences* by James Kalbach and *Journey Maps: The Tool for Design Innovation* by Robert Curedale.

CREATING WIREFRAMES

Now for the next Loop: *wireframing*. This is an easy way to show other people what you're thinking in terms of a workflow or the layout of the user interface (UI) of an application with just a few boxes and arrows on the whiteboard. It's also easy to make changes to what you've created when your team has feedback to consider.

Let's start with workflows. A workflow is similar to the User Journey Map in that it's intended to show the linear path someone can take through a product to accomplish a task. There will probably be multiple workflows for any product because people need to do different things from time to time. Even the most basic app probably has a workflow for the thing the app is designed to do and another for getting to and updating settings. Both of these should be laid out, showing how users will move from screen to screen to get where they need to go.

Imagine this workflow for our taco delivery app. The scenario might be:

1. Nicole wants to order two tacos.
2. She wants one with chicken and the other with only veggies.
3. She wants them delivered to her home address.
4. She wants to pay with a credit card.

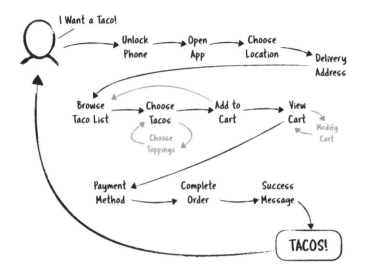

Wireframing is the process of defining what goes on each screen. The key to wireframing is to leave the details out. You just want to show the major parts of the interface. Things like navigation and screen titles can be nothing more than a box or a line. Don't get bogged down trying to make everything perfect. You just want to get the concepts on the wall so you can discuss them with the team and test to see that each workflow makes sense.

For example, if the workflow has you on a screen to take a photo, is there a button on that screen that allows you to take the photo? It sounds simple, but you'd be surprised how many mistakes you can find by simply walking through a workflow and thinking about what needs to be onscreen at each step of the process.

Back to our taco app, you'll probably want a screen where people can choose different types of tacos, a screen where they can choose toppings for the taco, a shopping cart screen where they can see the tacos they're ordering, a screen to enter the delivery address, a screen to enter payment info, maybe a screen to show delivery status, and so on.

Once you have a basic idea of what needs to be on each screen, you might want to invite some people from your target market in to make sure they understand what's happening and how your proposed process works. This can be very enlightening and expose some things that shape the future product in profound ways. Remember, *make mistakes when they're cheap and easy to recover from.* What's easier to recover from than erasing a box on a whiteboard and moving it to another place?

Now you've worked through the basic workflows and have an idea for what needs to be on which screen in the process, it's time to GOTO (Get Outta The Office) and go test this workflow in the outside world. Time to Loop back and do more Research.

DEVELOP A PAPER PROTOTYPE

The next Loop is to create a *Paper Prototype*, which is exactly what it sounds like. You're going sketch out what your solution would look like and how it would work on pieces of paper. You can even get fancy and buy notebooks in the size and shape of phones or tablets to make the whole thing feel more realistic.

As you work, remember these principles:

- Keep it low-fidelity (meaning "good enough to test broad concepts").
- Keep it low cost—don't sink a lot of time into making it look perfect.

You're basically going to copy what you've drawn on the whiteboard on sheets of paper and put them in the order they need to be for the workflow you're going to test. Start by drawing the major elements from each screen on a sheet and number the sheet according to where it falls in the workflow and put it in a stack for that workflow.

Pro Tip: If you're using the same screen in multiple workflows, create multiple sheets for it. This will help you keep things in order later without pulling sheets from one stack into another. It's also a good idea to keep several blank sheets with each stack so you can easily draw up a quick improv variation of that screen while you're testing with your target market.

Once you have all the stacks together, you're ready to go test. Tell people you're showing them an incomplete, proof of concept when you hand them a Paper Prototype. They won't be disappointed if what you show them doesn't function like a real app. Explain the basics of the elements on each screen so they understand what everything is supposed to do. However simple your prototype, its only job is to convey the basic idea for your solution and the value it offers the customer.

Tell them it's a way to help them accomplish a task, give them the scenario, and ask them to use the prototype to try to accomplish it. Then step back a little and observe how they respond. Remember what I told you about removing bias back in the User Research phase? **Don't help them!**

Our scenario:

1. Nicole wants to order two tacos.
2. She wants one with chicken and the other with only veggies.

3. She wants them delivered to her home address.
4. She wants to pay with a credit card.

Don't help them when they get stuck! Watch what they do, then if you see them struggling, ask, "Are you looking for something?" or "Is there something missing?" These questions allow them to tell you what they're expecting but not finding or understanding. Sometimes it's a matter of a button or some info being in the wrong location on the screen; sometimes they just get lost in the process.

This can be tricky, and it might be frustrating to you when you don't get the answers you're expecting. Just try to understand what has them stuck. This is a great time to whip out one of those blank sheets of paper, hand them a pen, and ask, "How would you prefer to see this work?" You'll be amazed at how some people will create a quick, crude sketch you can use to improve how the product works right there on the spot. The best thing? It only costs you a few minutes of your time and a simple sheet of paper. That's how you make cheap mistakes!

For more, check out *Paper Prototyping: The Fast and Easy Way to Design and Refine User Interfaces* by Carolyn Snyder.

DIGITAL PROTOTYPES

After a few Loops with Paper Prototypes, you'll want to

create a *Digital Prototype* (some people call them "clickable prototypes") so you can make it look more like a real product and test with more people. This takes significantly more work than whiteboarding or Paper Prototypes, so don't start creating Digital Prototypes until you're pretty confident you're on the right track.

A great tool to start creating Digital Prototypes is Axure (www.axure.com). It's a powerful tool that allows you to quickly get elements on a screen and publish to a website where other people can see it and play with it. The basics are pretty simple. It comes with UI elements like boxes, buttons, headings, text, and form fields. You can just drag them onto the screen in the position you want and click Publish. You can create actions on various elements to simulate your workflow, like clicking navigation links to go to different screens, clicking buttons to perform tasks, and more. It's a great way to build a simulated workflow and test with real people.

When you're ready to make something that looks and feels even more like a real product, tools like InVision, Figma, Framer, and Proto.io are all great. Tools like this make it easy to create rich visual interfaces that look and act like a live working product.

There is a lot more to using these tools. Healthy design organizations of all sizes have them at the very center of their process, which we'll get into again in the last section of this book.

For now, if you'd like to read more about creating and using Digital Prototypes, I recommend *Prototyping: A Practitioner's Guide* by Todd Zaki Warfel.

MAILCHIMP BUILDS A WEB APP

When Mailchimp looked at the types of customers who had the problem they validated during the research phase, they were mainly corporate marketers with a moderate level of technological sophistication. These were not people who'd be afraid to use software, whether they had to download it or log in online to use it. Consequently, Mailchimp's main concern when prototyping their solution was what would be easiest to build, deploy, test, maintain, and improve quickly. They settled on a web app over downloadable software for those reasons.

The web app they created allowed users to log in and choose from basic email templates Mailchimp knew would render correctly no matter the device or email provider. They allowed users to have control over basic things like images and text, but they didn't throw the kitchen sink of configuration possibilities at them. They built the simplest app possible that delivered value to their customers.

As more people used the app, Mailchimp got valuable feedback that allowed them to continuously improve the product. When they heard suggestions from users, they asked, "How might we solve this?" then they kept going through the Loops to ideate, prototype, and test new features and functionality.

Mailchimp is now one of the most valuable email marketing platforms on the planet. Want that kind of success? Keep reading. We're about to jump into the next big Loop.

Chapter Four

STEP THREE: TESTING

"I have not failed. I've just found 10,000 ways that won't work."

THOMAS EDISON

At this point in their evolution, Mailchimp had a simple web app where customers could log in and use a handful of templates to send a great looking email to their list. Customers had the ability to add images and text, but other than that, the interface was pretty basic because Mailchimp didn't yet know what their customers wanted. Their initial launch was far from a finished product. In truth, products are never finished. Software is never "done." More on that later.

As soon as they launched the first version of the web app, Mailchimp started asking customers for feedback. They looked at customer requests to find problem areas and features that were missing. The web app we know today is the result of hundreds, maybe thousands, of iterations of the Mailchimp team prototyping, testing, and refining their solution. Sometimes they had requests that only made sense for a small handful of users—and therefore never got added—while some updates were delivered to everyone.

As the requests came in, Mailchimp would build a simple prototype that delivered the requested functionality or value to their customer. They then went back to the users who requested it and asked how it worked for them.

They repeated the process we'll discuss in this chapter (and still do to this day).

A SERIES OF LOOPS

Now that you've finished the first Loop of the prototyping phase, you're ready for testing...right?

Well, yes and no. You see, prototyping and testing are iterative and comingle quite a lot. You'll constantly be looping back and forth between these phases. I've broken them into *phases* in this book, but it's really more like *mindsets*. You have to alternate between a *creative* mindset of ideation, wireframing, and prototyping to an *analytical* mindset of testing, observing, and measuring results. That's the only true path to success.

> You also may have noticed there's a lot of overlap between the *creative versus analytical mindsets* and the *divergent versus convergent thinking* we discussed earlier. If so, you're starting to see how all this fits together.

After you launch the first version of your product, you'll begin to receive feedback. You'll need to evaluate what people tell you and make decisions on what to do next. This starts the smaller Loops of tweaking the prototype, getting more feedback, tweaking again, and so on.

Remember, Human-Centered Business Design is not a straight path but a series of Loops. That goes for every phase, not just these two. To build a product people love, you must be prepared to move forward and backward between all phases or mindsets of this process at any given time.

When you sit down to test a Paper Prototype with a customer, you might loop between phases two and three on the fly as you move boxes around based on their feedback. This is the fun part, though! Don't be afraid of having customers pick apart your solution. You want that feedback now, while the prototypes are still cheap and easy to tweak.

Don't get discouraged if you burn through dozens of potential solutions. As long as you're making improvements based on validated user feedback, you'll be getting closer to finding the solution that customers will pay for because they see the value. Lots of people get discouraged and quit too soon when they don't get the answers they want to hear. Others jump in to explain how the solution works rather than letting it speak for itself, tainting the feedback from the customer and giving them false confidence in their potential solution.

You have to go into this process with a mindset that your current solution is one of many possibilities. There may be dozens of other solutions you just haven't thought of yet, but you won't know that until you get out and test your solution with customers. When you do, hand them the prototype and step back. Watch what they do and listen to what they say.

It's not your job to guide or train people on using your solution. If your long-term goal is to have a million customers, you can't personally train all of them. After all, nobody was trained how to use Google, Instagram, or Airbnb. If you want to scale a business, your product must stand on its own without explanation. If someone testing your prototype can't figure out how to use it on their own now, they're not going to figure it out later. If you have to jump in and show someone how to use what you built, you're doing yourself a disservice.

JUST RELEASE IT!

We've talked about wireframing and building Paper Prototypes to test your potential solutions. There's another way that I won't ignore, even if I don't recommend it for everybody: just release your solution into the wild and see what happens. Set up a simple landing page or a basic application, and see how the masses respond to it. Do they take action?

Here's an example. On your computer, when you copy and paste, you can only have one thing on your clipboard at a time. Whatever you copied last is the thing that will paste when you hit Ctrl+V (or Command+V). A company we worked with wanted to make a simple clipboard manager where you could keep more than one thing on your clipboard. When you go to copy and paste text, you can launch a little menu and choose from the last hundred things that you copied and paste whichever item you need.

To test this solution, the team created an image of the application (so it looked real) and posted it online with the message: *Coming soon. Preorder now for a 50% discount.*

They advertised to creative people like writers, designers, and coders who routinely use their clipboard. After receiving a ton of preorders in a short period of time, the team knew they had a winner and used that money to fund the creation of the application. It's now a successful app with hundreds of thousands of users.

If you understand a problem and a market well enough to already have a ton of confidence, there's nothing wrong with advertising your solution to see if customers will bite. If you're providing a service, you can do it manually, like Adaptly did, until you have the funds to write the software. If it's a product and you can't fake it, just say it's coming soon and let people preorder or give you an email address for a discount when it's released. People do that with books all the time. Why not do it with software?

One time with CoffeeCup Software, we had a new app coming out in three months. We released news about the software and showed some screenshots and mock-ups of what the software was going to do.

We publicized the release date and offered a 60 percent discount to people who ordered it three months ahead of the release, a 30 percent discount to those who ordered two months ahead, and 15 percent off for those who ordered at least ten days ahead of release. People preordered it, and that's what funded the development of the software.

Granted, we already had a mailing list of millions of people, so we had a captive audience that knew the software we built would be a good value. But the principle is the same: if you understand a problem well enough and can articulate a good Value Proposition, nothing stops you from going ahead and releasing it. If nobody takes you up on the offer, then you're probably wrong about something. You've got the wrong market, the wrong Value Proposition, or you're solving the wrong problem. Then you have to go back to the drawing board. The good news is you didn't spend lots of time and money creating something nobody wants.

It's a risk to tell people you can do something you can't do yet, but this option can work if you know your problem and your market, and can articulate the value of your solution.

So how do you decide what to test and how to test it? Read on...

HYPOTHESIS GRID

A hypothesis grid is a useful tool for testing your prototype. Once you start getting feedback from customers and wanting to test the ideas they give you, this framework will guide your experiments and help explain the results. Let's take a look:

YOUR HUNCH

ASSUMPTIONS:	HYPOTHESIS:
EXPERIMENTS:	RESULTS:

To download a copy of the Hypothesis Grid, visit Loopsbook.com/resources.

There are five sections on the hypothesis grid, starting with the idea you're testing. In the upper left quadrant, you'll list your assumptions. What are you assuming about the world of your customers and how might they respond to this idea? In the upper right quadrant is space for your hypothesis: *If we do _____, then ___ percent of people will do _____.*

The bottom left quadrant is where you describe your experiment and how you'll measure to judge the success of the experiment.

The bottom right quadrant asks perhaps the most important questions:

What did you learn? What will you do next?

Armed with this information, you can loop back to the prototyping phase to tweak your solution and come back to the customer with another idea to test.

Here's an example of the process at work. When Amazon wants to improve something, like the number of people who add a suggested item to their cart, they follow a process very similar to what we've discussed so far. They'll have ideation sessions to come up with a few ways they might be able to make improvements, build a few prototypes, define what they are going to change and how they'll measure whether it worked.

KNOW IT LIKE THE BACK OF YOUR HAND

When you meet with a customer and present your potential solution for them to test, you don't want to be confused, keep referring to your notes, or wildly click around your wireframe because you forgot how the User Journey unfolds. Not only will this give the customer an immediate negative impression, they'll also feed off your confusion.

You should have the process so clearly defined in your head that you can talk about it without looking at a single note or prop. Better yet, if your laptop dies while you're in the middle of testing, or you don't have your laptop handy when you bump into a potential customer, you should be able to sketch it out on paper and explain it without missing a step. That's how well you should know the User Journey and Value Proposition.

Remember, you're not rehearsing so you can coach the customer through your potential solution, holding their hand every step of the way. This is about being able to present the potential solution in a way the customer can understand what it's meant to do and so you can answer any questions they may have while evaluating it. You can't help them understand what you're trying to build if you don't understand every aspect of it yourself.

REVISIT AND RECRUIT TEST CUSTOMERS

Now your Wireframes and Paper Prototypes are ready to test, you've got your hypothesis grids for the experiments you want to test, you've mapped the User Journey, and you've rehearsed your presentation—now it's time to get out there and start getting feedback! The first step is to follow up with the people you talked to during interviews in the research phase. You've built a rapport with these people, you know they have the problem you're trying to solve, and since you asked to follow up with them, they're expecting you to bring them a solution to test. *You kept their contact info, right?*

In addition to revisiting the people you talked to in the research phase, bring in new people as well. Use the same recruitment strategies we discussed in Chapter 2. If you're running a Facebook or Craigslist ad, don't worry too much about demographics or psychographics. You're just trying to send up a dog whistle for people who have this problem.

Let's say you're posting to find people to interview about a real estate app. You'd probably want to post under Community > General Community. You could also post under Gigs > Computer Gigs. It's free to post, so try a few sections to see what works best for you.

Here's a Craigslist ad template you can use. Feel free to tweak it for your needs:

Posting title: Real Estate sales survey - $10 Amazon gift card

Posting body: I'm working on a new business idea that will help make it easier for realtors to manage their contacts, and I want to better understand how realtors are doing this today.

If you're a realtor and you've been frustrated with managing contact and feel like there might be a better way, please email me with a short 1-2 sentence description of how you manage your contacts, and we can set up a time to talk for 15-20 minutes. In return, you'll get a $10 Amazon gift card.

Thanks!

A few things to keep in mind when posting ads:

1. Where you put the ad will introduce some biases. For example: location (because you pick a city or multiple cities to post) and which category you post in.
2. Most people respond at night when they aren't working, so expect at least a one-day delay before emails come in.
3. Make sure you're clear in your posting what the requirements are. A few people who don't fit the criteria might email you, so you should come up with ways to filter them out before scheduling an interview.
4. If you feel like you're not getting enough responses, consider increasing your incentive. A high level of compensation is $1 per minute of time you're asking them for, but I'd suggest starting a little lower at first, as very few people make $60/hour.
5. Don't forget to factor in no-shows. For example, I

posted a Craigslist ad like the sample we saw earlier for realtors in a handful of cities and in the course of a week, I had twenty interviews scheduled. Only six people (30 percent) actually showed up, even after accepting the meeting invite. I'd recommend following up the day before or the morning of to confirm they're coming and remind them of the incentive.

Set meetings with people, present them with the solution prototype, ask them to attempt to complete a simple task (one from the Hypothesis Grid), and let them play with the prototype. Your job is to remain a neutral observer. If they have questions, answer them. Take notes on everything—how they use the prototype, what they like, where they get stuck, the questions they ask, what they thought would happen, what they would change, etc.

HOW MANY PEOPLE SHOULD YOU TALK TO?

All of them. You can't talk to too many people. You can talk to the wrong people, but you can't talk to too many of the right people. The more people who test your solution and give you feedback, the greater chance you have of success.

Think of it like investigating a crime that happened in a public space with a hundred witnesses nearby. After you talk to five people, you'll have a good idea of what happened. Talk to twenty people and that idea will become clearer. But you must talk to every witness because the last person you interview might crack the case wide open for you!

That's the value of interviews—every piece of feedback can adjust your course.

Remember the Curve of Despair? As you talk to more and more people, you might get discouraged because a common thread hasn't emerged yet. Keep going! Talk to more people. More information is always better than less information. Yes, it can feel paralyzing to look at all the information you've gathered and not see a clear way forward. Press on. The clarity will come.

TALK TO THE RIGHT PEOPLE

Keep in mind that it's important to test your solution with the right people. Talking to the wrong people will waste your time and send you off in the wrong direction. Even if the people you're talking to have the problem you're trying to solve, they may not be the best people to test your solution. Here's an example to show you what I mean.

If you were trying to make a better corkscrew to open a bottle of wine, who would you go to first: the grandma

HOW TO REQUEST FEEDBACK ON A PROTOTYPE

When the user has trouble with your prototype, use these questions to guide the discussion:

What were you trying to accomplish?

This explains the intention behind the user's actions.

What did you do?

This gives you the first indication of where things went wrong.

What did you expect to happen?

This can illuminate a few things: a flawed assumption you made, a missed step in your User Journey, or a missing feature that should be added.

What actually happened?

This shows you where the prototype failed and how it might be improved.

Here's an example of how a customer will give feedback:

"What were you trying to accomplish?"

"I was trying to add an image to my email."

"What did you do?"

"Well, I clicked on this thing over here and I dragged it."

"What did you expect to happen?"

"I expected to see the image drop into my email, but the image disappeared."

who has a bottle of wine once a month or the bartender who opens multiple bottles a night? You're looking for the person with the acute pain (meaning the pain is intense and sharply focused), not the person who occasionally has the problem.

The "right people" are the people with deep pain points around this problem. They may not feel those pain points multiple times a day, but when they do, it hurts like hell.

When you test your new corkscrew with bartenders, don't stop after you've talked to ten of them. There are thousands of bartenders in the world, and while your solution might work for one bartender, they might be the only person in the world who opens bottles that way. Or maybe you only tested the corkscrew with right-handed bartenders. When you give the corkscrew to a left-handed bartender, you find out it cuts their finger. That's a big problem with your prototype, but if you don't talk to enough people, you might never find it.

If you test the prototype with eighty bartenders and fifty of them fumble with it, that's a good sign you need to go back to the drawing board. But if fifty of them ask to keep your prototype at the end of the night, you might have found the right solution.

The smart reader may have noticed a "gotcha" buried in that last example. I said a "better" corkscrew, but I didn't say what makes it "better" nor did I say what problem we are trying to solve with the corkscrew.

If we're trying to open bottles faster, bartenders might be the best people to talk to. But if we're trying to make it easier to hold and safer to use, you'd probably want to talk to grandma. The same corkscrew might solve both problems, and that's great. You would test different things with each person relative to the problem they have. You have to make sure the person you're talking to has the problem you're trying to solve.

HOW TO DEAL WITH BUYING SIGNALS

It's easy to have two or three interviews in a row go well and think everything is awesome and you should just go for it. But you have to keep the size of the market in mind and make sure you've talked to a representative chunk of that market. Like the research phase, the only way to overcome the Curve of Despair is to keep collecting knowledge and feedback.

The more people you talk to, the more confidence you gain. If you're consistently seeing a lot of the people you talk to like your idea, that's a good signal. You can also gain confidence from the intensity of somebody's reaction. If they're lukewarm about your solution, that's an indication. If you have a solid 30 percent of people who think your product is awesome and want to give you money immediately, then figure out what is similar about that 30 percent of customers and hone in on that market.

These indications are called *buying signals*. When people

start asking about release dates or want to pay upfront, there are two takeaways worth noting. First, the confidence in your potential solution goes up. The customer understands how your solution works and sees the value it offers. Second, you'll get an idea of what customers might pay. If someone wants to buy the solution right then, ask them what they think it's worth and write it down. Their answer doesn't determine your price, but it will help with your pricing decisions.

When people treat your prototype with skepticism or hesitancy, try to figure out what's going on. Don't assume the worst. Sometimes people are skeptical because they're confused or their pain just isn't acute enough to see value in the solution. If your prototype is met with a generally skeptical look, you may have missed the mark (at least for that person).

Be careful with customers at the extremes—those who love your solution and those who hate it. There will be people who don't get what you're trying to do. It's fine. Understand why they don't get it, but you don't need to talk to them anymore because they'll probably never be your customer. At the other end, don't put too much stock into the person who loves your solution. They might be the loudest person in the room, and as we all know, the squeaky wheel tends to get the grease. If you focus in on that one person (not one *type* of person), you run the risk of tailoring the product to a group of people too small to build a business around. Remember, you're trying to find a group of people large enough that it will make sense to invest in building the product. Otherwise, you'll be on a fool's errand.

LOOKING OUTSIDE THE MARKET

Another group you'll encounter during testing is outliers. These are the folks who don't fit one of your established roles and weren't on your radar to interview, yet somehow found out about your solution. Think back to our real estate example from earlier. If you designed an app to replace the spreadsheets that real estate brokers were using for lead follow-up, you might be surprised when a commercial real estate broker shows real interest.

At this point, the commercial real estate broker is an outlier. Your target audience was residential brokers who sell houses worth more than $400,000, yet this broker is selling buildings with over 100,000 square feet and price tags in the millions. He's not in your original target market, yet he's offering to pay for your solution right now. What should you do with these people?

The first option is to set them aside and focus on your target market. You don't want to get distracted and end up down a rabbit hole just because one person showed interest.

The other option is to figure out what role the outlier fills (what is *their* pain point?) and look for other actors who fit that role. It might be worth doing some interviews to see if this one broker was alone in his enthusiasm or if there's a bigger market out there that you hadn't thought about. Research will show if your outlier is an anomaly or a signal of a bigger, adjacent market that you can serve without altering the product much.

Which option to choose? That's a function of time. How much time do you have to pursue another potential market right now? Probably not a lot. It's usually—*but not always*—better to stay focused on the original market since you've already done so much research into it. Absolutely stay in contact with the commercial real estate broker and come back to them once you've proven you can or can't get traction with the residential brokers. They could be either an additional market segment or your first pivot.

NEEDS BUYERS AND ECONOMIC BUYERS

Not all buyers are the same. In every transaction, big or small, you have an *economic buyer*, the person who makes the money decision, and you have the *needs buyer*, the person who needs their problem solved. Sometimes these buyers are the same person, sometimes they are multiple people. For example, if you're buying new running shoes or a language translation app for yourself, you are both the needs buyer and the economic buyer. But if you're buying something for your spouse, you're just the economic buyer. Your spouse is the needs buyer (even if it's a gift).

In a B2C situation, you can be reasonably confident the person you're talking to is both the needs and economic buyer. There are always exceptions, but more often than not, consumers are buying things they need, things that address problems they have, or are at least affected by in some way.

In a B2B situation, the needs buyer is rarely the economic buyer. Think about an auditor who needs your new software to better manage their books. They might love your app, but they don't have the buying power—the purchasing manager or someone in accounting or supply chain does.

It's rare in B2B settings that the needs buyer and the economic buyer are the same person, especially in a bigger company. An executive with P&L responsibility could potentially be both buyers, but even they will typically have other people who influence the decision. If you're talking to a Director or Vice President, they're probably going to ask their managers if your product is something that will be used if it solves the problem. As an executive, they're typically no longer a true needs buyer anymore, but they recognize the importance of getting input from the real needs buyers, the people on their team who will actually use your solution.

When you do interviews, you have to understand which of the two buyers you're talking to so you can formulate the Value Proposition correctly. Typically, you'll be talking to the needs buyer because you are focused on solving a problem.

However, once you return to the market to validate your solution, you've got to pay attention to whether the person you're talking to is the needs buyer, the economic buyer, or both. Much like offering both features and benefits, you've got to appeal to both groups if you want to make the sale.

> Pro Tip: Ask the person you're interviewing who makes the purchasing decisions at their company. Their answer will tell you if they are the economic buyer, the needs buyer, or both.

THE PERPETUAL VALIDATION LOOP

You're going to loop back and forth between prototyping and testing, so what happens when it feels like you're not getting any traction? This will probably happen. Don't panic. When you're stuck in a perpetual loop, it's usually because you're not getting clear feedback. This isn't your potential customers' fault. You're probably not asking the right questions during testing.

Remember the Washington Monument story? If you're trying to stop the deterioration by designing a better detergent, you're never going to solve the real problem. You might need to dig a little deeper in your research to understand what's truly going on if the feedback you're getting sends you back to the drawing board over and over again.

Another thing that can cause this perpetual loop is when you fall in love with your idea and fall out of love with the problem. You risk falling in love with the solution when you don't understand the problem well enough. You might have an idea for a really awesome app, but every time you go out and talk to people about the app, no one is interested because you're not solving the right problem. Yet you keep searching for people who "get it" instead of "getting it" yourself. In that case, you're a hammer in search of a nail. You've got a thing that nobody wants because you're trying to solve a problem nobody has, at least not the people you've talked to. You need to loop back to the beginning and make yourself understand the problems people have.

Not refining the market well enough will also keep you

stuck in a loop. Back to our real estate example, maybe you're chasing big-city brokers when it's actually small-town brokers who have the problem. But you didn't discover that fact earlier because you didn't do the right research, or enough of it. Or maybe the problem isn't staying in touch with existing clients; the problem is finding new clients. In that case, you had the wrong problem.

As I said before, a lot of startup people call this product/market fit. I like to flip it around and call it market/product fit because I want you to focus on the market first. When people focus on the product first, they tend to fall in love with the solution instead of the problem.

If I wanted to build a better mousetrap, I'd talk to a bunch of people who have a problem with mice, and I'd do experiments to see what kind of trap would work for them. You wouldn't come up with some contraption with no validation and try to sell it to them. The concept of creating a product first and then trying to sell it is from the seller-driven economy of yesteryear. As you now know, in a buyer-driven economy, building products people love starts with asking what people want.

As scary as it is, if you find yourself unable to escape a perpetual loop, go back to the very beginning. Do your research again, make a new prototype, and get back in the market.

There's no hard and fast rule for the right number of Loops you'll do before it's time to go back to step 1. This is a messy process. It's more alchemy than science. You might have enough confidence in just three Loops to know your potential solution isn't working. You might be twenty Loops in and gaining confidence, then realize it isn't happening, and head back to step 1 to regroup. It all depends on how well you understand the problem and how well your potential solution addresses it.

MAILCHIMP PLAYED IT SMART

One of the wise moves Mailchimp made early on was investing in Design Operations to help them make their ideas a reality. The people they hired understood the design process from both a visual and an interactive perspective, and they knew how to communicate design decisions to both the engineering and business teams. They also hired researchers to make sure they were staying connected to their customers' needs. This was instrumental in making sure customer feedback was the main driver of product updates.

For example, Jenn Downs, who led the research team at the time, pioneered a method of watching users use the mobile app to understand how they approached various tasks. You're probably familiar with video conferencing where you can see the person you're talking to. What Jenn did was brilliant. She asked the customer to hold their laptop backward in their lap so the camera is facing the phone instead of their face. This way the researcher can observe how the user interacts with the app in real time.

They found other new ways of doing user research to confirm their prototypes were of value to users. After they had enough research to build confidence that the changes or additions to the app actually delivered value to their customers, they updated the product.

In Mailchimp's Loop, the research team figured out what people needed. The design team joined in for step 2 and made the prototypes, then handed them back to the research team to test the revised prototypes with real users. Finally, an analytics team looked at those tests and provided feedback to the design and research teams on what worked and what didn't. By creating a communication cycle early on, Mailchimp leveraged these three teams to quickly process customer requests and customer feedback, and to improve the product.

You may not have the ability to hire a research team, a design team, and an analytics team, but you can shift your frame of mind between those three things: doing research to identify problems, prototyping and testing solutions, and analyzing the results. Those are the Loops.

If you can successfully loop between those mindsets and do accurate, unbiased research, understand customer needs, come up with creative ways to deliver value, build simple, low-cost prototypes, and validate your prototypes through testing, then you're on the road to building a product people will buy, use, and love.

Let's look at where that road leads next: branding and positioning.

LET'S DO IT!

Have you ever tried to ride a unicycle? It's *extremely* difficult to stay balanced, let alone ride it in a straight line. You have to maintain balance, steer the wheel in the right direction, and provide power to get there all through one tiny contact point between the tire and the ground. Identifying a problem, building a product to solve it, and building a company around that product is a lot like riding a unicycle—in both cases, you have one point of contact with the earth. Starting out, your product is all you have to balance, steer, give direction, and provide the power to get somewhere. Like I said, it's not easy!

Once you get up and moving and the longer you ride a unicycle, you'll gain more confidence in your abilities. The same is true here. You've done the work of validating the problem you saw, designing a solution, then testing and refining that solution to the point that you have confidence it solves your customer's problem.

Congratulations! You have the balance of confidence in your product, and you can see the direction to go, which gives you the power to start going there. Now you're ready to graduate to a bicycle. It's much easier to ride a bicycle because you have two wheels, two points of contact. Think of the front wheel as your product and the discipline you've built in the first three Loops, and the back wheel as the business you're going to build to push that product forward and to get where you want to go. Loops 4 and 5 cover two fundamental pieces of creating a business around your product: (1) building a brand and (2) building products with speed and scale.

I often get asked why branding and positioning come now, after all these Loops of creating the product and before the Loop of building at speed. Simple: without developing a Brand Ethos and a Brand Identity with guidelines on how to use them, you won't have any direction for how things look or how to talk to your customers. With no brand, you have no consistency. You can start building your product concurrently with your brand, but you can't complete your product until your brand is established. Before you plant your flag in the ground and start selling your product, people have to know who you are. It's better if this work is done before you have a product to sell because then you'll be ready to launch quickly.

You've got your plan, you know what you're building, now it's time to execute—let's do it!

Chapter Five

STEP FOUR: BRANDING AND POSITIONING

"Brands are all about trust. That trust is built in drops and lost in buckets."

KEVIN PLANK, FOUNDER AND CEO, UNDER ARMOUR

Mailchimp's brand began as a manifestation of the two founders' personalities. Ben and Dan wanted something that was human and relatable, that didn't take itself too seriously, but that was still business-oriented. If you recall, one of the things Rocket Science Group did for their customers was send marketing postcards on their behalf. The name Mailchimp actually came from one of their most popular marketing postcards, and their original logo looked a lot like clip art. Every aspect of their brand was meant to reinforce the idea that Mailchimp was approachable, fun, and friendly.

In other words, it was built for humans.

Mailchimp's brand stands in stark contrast to their competitors with names like Campaign Monitor, Constant Contact, Hubspot, and Infusionsoft. Not very friendly or approachable company names. As we'll see, a company's name is not its entire brand, but if you were a small business owner deciding between those options, my guess is you'd be drawn to Mailchimp because it sounds less intimidating and a little fun.

In the rest of this chapter, we'll see how everything your brand comprises should help position you to stand out from the competition and set you up for success.

A BRAND IS MORE THAN A LOGO

The first known brand was an engraving found on a cork from a bottle of oil in ancient Mesopotamia that dated back to around 3000 BC. In those times, Mesopotamian traders would bring bottles of oil to market with their brand on it, and buyers knew they were getting oil that had an established level of quality, taste, and price.

The modern usage of the word "brand" comes from branding cattle. Ranchers would burn markings into the sides of their cattle to show who owns the cow and where it comes from when it's brought to market. The brands also helped in the case of cattle rustlers stealing livestock from ranchers. There's no doubt who those cows belong to.

Let's say I have a large, grass-fed cattle ranch called Double J, and I brand my cattle with my Double J logo. When my cattle come to market, you can see my logo and know that the cattle come from a large ranch and are grass-fed. There's a certainty a logo provides to consumers. It's a mark that distinguishes products from other products.

This is where the misconception of a logo being a brand originated. A brand goes much deeper than just a logo.

> A brand exists at the intersection of what your company does and how people feel about it.

Everything that goes into your brand gives people an idea of the quality of the product or the experience they're going to have.

Think about Coca-Cola, which is arguably the largest, most recognized brand on the planet. The first half of the equation (what Coca-Cola does) is obvious: they make beverages. What's funny is that the way people feel about Coca-Cola—the Brand Affinity—has changed throughout the decades, and the company has had to respond to these changes. As people have recently become more health-conscious, you've seen Coca-Cola shift their products accordingly. They purchased *Dasani*, a bottled water brand. They started making *Coke Zero* to appeal to people who were concerned about calories. They created *Coca-Cola Life*, which is sweetened with cane sugar instead of high-fructose corn syrup. All of these changes in product are the result of changing customer demand. You see, even the biggest brands in the world have to listen to their customers or risk losing them.

Brand Affinity can also shift with zero changes to the packaging or product.

Take Tesla for example, a brand everyone is hot on right now. It's understandable—they make sexy electric cars and invent cool technology. But what if Tesla batteries started blowing up while people were driving and people died? Tesla's Brand Affinity would be badly hurt, without any changes to the logo, name, or product.

A brand is not only the name or the logo. Those things matter, but ultimately, your brand is what your company does and how your customers feel about it. If you keep that in mind, you'll be able to create a stronger brand that resonates with your target market. A stronger brand will allow you to build trust and do more than you ever imagined because customers more easily and willingly buy from a brand they trust.

FIRST IMPRESSIONS OF YOUR BRAND

When you start to think about your brand, imagine how you'd want it personified. If your brand was a person and they walked into the room right now, what would you say about them? How would you describe them?

What do they look like? How are they dressed? How do they act? How do they carry themselves? How do they talk?

Tall or short? Wearing a suit or swim trunks?

Authoritative or more laid back?

Reserved and shy? Or vibrant and boisterous?

Casual and using slang, maybe with some type of accent, or using words and phrases that are proper and articulate?

These types of physical and personality characteristics create a first impression when we meet someone. It's the same with your brand. What do you want the first impression of your brand to be? This might seem silly, but remember that you're designing products for humans, which means your brand must connect with people when they see it for the first time. If your brand personality is distinguished, academic, reserved, and with an intimidating vocabulary, you might not do very well selling urban streetwear to teenagers.

If your brand was a person, would your customers want to get coffee, lunch, or a beer with them and hang out? Could your brand and your customer be friends? You want to create a bond with your customer that feels natural and complementary.

At the same time, a good brand personality doesn't *duplicate* the customer—it's *compatible* with the customer. You don't want to mirror the customer because many people don't like looking in a mirror. They want to relate to your brand but also picture themselves in a better place because of what you offer, which means you want to be a bit aspirational.

As you start to think about the personality, you'll want to dig deep and identify ways to describe your *Brand Ethos*. A Brand Ethos is a set of words or phrases that describe what your brand is and is not. These words and phrases define the characteristics and personality of your brand in a way that help make it real and provides a reference for all future decisions about how your brand acts. It will become the cornerstone you build your brand upon.

HOW TO DEVELOP YOUR BRAND ETHOS

For this activity, you're going to need a stack of cards with different personality traits written on them that might describe your brand. You'll also need some blank cards or sticky notes for later in the process.

The cards have contrasting—but not necessarily opposite—concepts on each side. For example: a card says "mass-market" on one side and "niche" on the other. Another says "timeless" on one side and "current" on the other. Another says "certain" on one side and "curious" on the other.

You can make these cards yourself (time-consuming) or just buy them online. Check out Loopsbook.com/resources to see some of the decks we recommend. The decks we use have about fifty cards, with 100 contrasting concepts. This gives us nearly limitless possibilities for defining a Brand Ethos.

Once you have the cards, gather your team around a big table. On this table, create four zones: *We Are*, *We Are Not*, *I'm Not Sure*, and *Does Not Apply*. Distribute all the cards evenly between everyone on the team. Just deal them out like you're playing Go Fish.

ARE	UNSURE	ARE NOT

Next, everyone on the team will quietly look at each card they have, think about which side of the card is more applicable, and place it in one of the zones. This takes a bit of thought.

As you look at each card, consider whether it's more important to be known by a trait (*We Are*) or not be known by a trait (*We Are Not*). The distinction may seem small, but it's important. For example, is it more important for your customer to know "We are niche" or "We are not mass market?" Do not talk to each other during this part of the exercise. Just place the cards where they feel right. We'll talk in the next phase.

Once all the cards are on the table, start with the *I'm Not Sure* zone. Look at each concept, discuss with your team, and decide if there's a similar concept that better articulates your brand in the *We Are* or *We Are Not* zones. For example, "big" might be in the *I'm Not Sure* zone, but when you look over at the *We Are* zone, you see "bold," which is a better fit for your brand.

To discard a concept from the *I'm Not Sure* pile—or replace a card in the *We Are* or *We Are Not* zone with a card from *I'm Not Sure*, you must have a unanimous vote. If it's not unanimous, keep discussing! Eventually, the team will agree what to do. This discussion and debate is exactly what the exercise is about. It's forcing you to discuss, as a team, what personality you want your brand to have. It's important to explore all the nuance between what seem like similar concepts. That's how you get to the true essence of the brand.

After you finish with the *I'm Not Sure* zone, start organizing similar concepts in the *We Are Not* zone. For example, "technical" and "scientific" might go together. Once you're done organizing the *We Are Not* zone, do the same for the *We Are* zone. When you finish, take a step back and survey what you have. Now is actually a good time to take a quick coffee/water break.

With all the remaining cards in the *We Are* or *We Are Not* zones, you're ready for an open discussion about which concepts are most important to your brand and most accurately describe it. It's typical to have more *We Are* traits since people tend to focus more on the positive than the negative. I advise teams to start with the *We Are* zone and keep an eye on the *We Are Not* zone as you go and discuss any potential similarities or conflicts as they come up.

As you go through this process, prioritize the concepts that feel most true to your brand and eliminate the ones that don't feel as important or accurate. You should get down to a couple dozen in each zone at this point, which is when the hard part begins! At this point, a third-party moderator or facilitator can be extremely helpful to keep things on track and make sure the discussion stays focused on the outcome, rather than debating semantics. Ideally you need to narrow it down to ten or fewer personality traits in the *We Are* zone, and six or fewer in the *We Are Not* zone.

Start with large concept groups and work your way down to smaller ones. For each cluster, no matter how big, get down to the one concept that best says what the cluster represents. You don't need unanimous votes here, but you can't have an adamant dissenter. Sometimes the cluster of words is really close to the right concept, but it's not exactly right. This is a good time to break out a thesaurus and your sticky notes. Work together to find the word or phrase that fits *exactly*. Remember, this will become the ethos that drives all your other brand activities, so invest the time and effort to get it right.

Once you get down to the right number of concepts for each zone, congratulations—that's your brand personality! For example, we did this exercise with a fintech startup. The list we ultimately ended up with was: We are *bold, clever, effective, insightful, personal, purposeful,* and *simple.* We are not *ordinary, exclusive, traditional,* and *subjective.*

From this list, you can get a pretty good idea what this brand is like and how it would be personified—how it would look, act, and speak if it walked in the room.

The reason we define the Brand Ethos first is because everything else that you build around the brand is going to reference that ethos. When you move on to the next step, naming your company, the name must be consistent with what you decided here.

Ask yourself, would the name Campaign Monitor work for a brand with a personality like Mailchimp's? Probably not.

NAMING YOUR COMPANY

Your name is a crucial part of your identity. It has to be

distinct, memorable, easy to spell and pronounce, and perhaps more importantly, unique enough to trademark. Plus, in some cases, your name is your logo. Think about IBM and FedEx. You need to find a name that embodies your Brand Ethos *and* communicates what you do or the value you provide. You could take a shot in the dark, or you could follow a proven process to find a name that you and your customers will love.

THE STRUGGLE IS REAL

I'm not going to lie, naming is hard. There are only so many words and concepts, and any language puts a lot of limitations on how words can be used and still make sense. Most of the best names are already taken. Whether it's in use by a competitor or just being held on the sidelines, you'll find it's difficult to get any common word as your brand name.

There are alternative ways to spell things, like how it was fashionable for startups to drop vowels from common words so they could buy an affordable domain name (a lot of the best domain names are already taken). Consider Flickr, Tumblr, and DSTLD. Not a terrible way to go, but not great either. Some words have multiple meanings or have slang equivalents that might get you in trouble. Unlike coming up with the name of your child, which can be an esoteric process driven by gut feelings, naming a company is a more scientific process driven by data and research.

Oh yikes, you're thinking, *this fun process now sounds super boring!*

Having gone through this dozens of times, I can personally attest that the naming process is actually really fun. You're going to look at direct competitors and complementary products to see how their names break down, then have a few sessions with your team to come up with something that truly represents your brand and connects with your audience.

Let's get started with competitor research to see what you're up against.

NAME STYLES

There are four styles of names: functional, invented, experiential, and evocative.

Functional names are purely descriptive of what a company or product does. For example, Craigslist is Craig's list of stuff. Meetup is where you go to meet up with other people. Ford Motor Company is named for its founder, Henry Ford.

Invented names can come from two origins: names built

on Greek or Latin roots, or names that are poetic constructions based on the rhythm and experience of saying them. Google is a good example of an invented name. It's similar to a mathematical term, but they changed it to be based on Greek and Latin roots. Firefox, Oreo, and Jeep are other examples of invented names.

Experiential names offer a direct connection to something real or to a part of the human experience. Gusto, Aquafresh, and Quicken are examples of experiential names that help you imagine or remember the experience you had with the product.

Evocative names are designed to evoke the position of a company or product rather than the goods or services provided. Pandora is an example of this. You imagine opening Pandora's box of music. Virgin, Mailchimp, Amazon, and Oracle are other examples.

NAME TAXONOMY STUDY

Now that you know the four styles of names, it's time for a name taxonomy study. Look at all the other company names and product names in the ecosystem where your product will live. Sort each company or product name into one of the four categories. Not all names will fit neatly into one category, so use your team's best judgment.

Once all the names are sorted into categories, rate them based on *energy level*. Sure, energy is a subjective measurement. Go with your gut. What sounds cool to you? Which names carry some energy? Is it fun to say or think about? Which ones are you drawn to? Which ones sound dull and boring?

Let's look at some names in the airline industry.

- Delta
- Jet Blue
- Air France
- American Airlines
- British Airways
- United

How would you rank these on the energy scale? My guess would be Jet Blue, United, Delta, British Airways, Air France, and American Airlines. Do this exercise yourself and see how you rank them. It will be good practice for later.

In the invented category, we have Qantas. It's a bit curious. What does Qantas mean? I don't know, but I wouldn't describe it as high-energy. The name Qantas just doesn't get me excited. In the evocative category, however, Virgin is right at the top. It's got a lot of energy and emotion tied in to the name.

Once you've compiled and sorted all the names in the ecosystem where your company and product will live, you want to lay them out on a matrix that has the four categories on the x-axis and an excitement scale on the y-axis that goes from –2 (low energy) to +5 (very high energy). Here's an example:

	FUNCTIONAL	INVENTED	EXPERIENTIAL	EVOCATIVE
5				
4				
3				
2				
1				
0				

To download a copy of the Name Taxonomy Matrix, visit Loopsbook.com/resources.

Plot out the names you identified, then see where there might be a gap. Maybe none of the companies have evocative names. Or maybe all the functional names are really low energy. The grid shows where an opportunity to differentiate yourself might exist.

Note: There is a subtle difference between naming a company and naming a product. This process can and should be used for both. If you're creating a startup, you'll probably use the same name for both, at least for now. If you're working on a product in an established company, you can still use this process to name the product. Just make sure it aligns with the company's brand ethos and standards.

THE NAMESTORM

The NameStorm is essentially two working sessions separated by at least a couple of days for the Soak. It's a challenging and fun part of the process. Think of it like a brainstorming session where you and your team will generate lots of ideas, then distill them down into a few good name candidates. Once again, you'll need a room with a large whiteboard (the bigger the better). It's best if you can use a room that won't be disturbed for a few days while the process unfolds. You'll also need several dry-erase markers, a thesaurus, spreadsheet software like Excel or Google Sheets, some snacks, and coffee.

NAMESTORM DAY ONE

On the first day, you'll use *divergent thinking* to generate ideas and concepts related to the company or product you're creating. Get your team into the room and write on the whiteboard all the words you can think of that relate to your brand personality. Don't be conservative.

You want to get as many words and phrases as possible on the whiteboard. Don't worry about where they are or try to group anything. Just write *everything* down. It will be sloppy and that's okay.

Have one of your team members capture each word or phase in a spreadsheet as you go. That will help eliminate duplicates, and it will speed up the next phase of the process.

Spend a solid two hours just coming up with words and phrases that somehow relate to what you're building. It's going to get hard, and you're going to get stuck. Eventually, the team is going to start slowing down, but you have to push through it. Think about how to say things in other languages. Think about roots of words in Latin and Greek, about slang and colloquialisms, about misspellings or weird combinations of words. Get out the thesaurus and explore other words related to what you've already written down. Nothing is out of bounds here. Think about everything you possibly can and get it up on the board.

It helps to have someone doing online research into words, phrases, and concepts at the same time. There are tons of ways to find related words, like Wikipedia, Thesaurus.com, Google Translate, and searching for related words.

EXPLORE WORD COMBINATIONS

When you combine words, some will make sense, and some won't. That's okay. Try odd combinations because sometimes you'll find something interesting. That's how names like "Hubspot," "Hootsuite," and frankly, "Mailchimp" came to be.

You're guaranteed to find some interesting word pairs if you just try everything on the board with everything else on the board. Most pairings won't make sense and some will be funny or just plain ridiculous. Keep going. You might find something fantastic in there.

PREFIXES AND SUFFIXES

English is interesting because you can use almost any word as a prefix or suffix. Other languages aren't as forgiving in this way. For example, if you're building a software product the word *soft* could be a great prefix or suffix. *Ware* and *tech* could also be good suffixes. Short, descriptive words like *up*, *top*, or *go* can be very interesting when paired with another word.

Let's say you're building a product designed to help stabilize tall buildings against high-speed winds. When you start looking at words related to the sky or being up, you find the Latin root word *levo*. With that in mind, you start thinking about what you can put with *levo* that makes sense: LevoScience, LevoSoft, and LevoTech all might be good candidates.

Also, a lot of companies use colors or animals to build their names, like Jet Blue, Red Bull, or Mailchimp. Think about a color or an animal that embodies your brand personality and use it as a prefix or suffix.

TRIMMING

Trimming syllables from words can also lead to interesting names. Let's say you're naming a product that helps people work at high altitudes and you have the word "altitude" on the board. It's a good word but doesn't communicate everything we need on its own. You pair it with *tech* as a suffix and have *AltitudeTech*. Reasonable name, but it might be even better by trimming it to *AltiTech*.

Pro Tip: You can run a formula in Excel that will put words from two columns into all the possible combinations so you can see what the pairs look like. This is great for word pairings or adding prefixes and suffixes. Just Google "Excel concatenation" to find step-by-step instructions on how to create and run this formula. This won't help with trimming, but it's a great start.

WRAPPING UP

When the first session is over, your whiteboard will be

covered edge to edge in a jumbled mess of words and phrases. Words will be everywhere, and it won't be coherent, and that's exactly what you want.

Make sure you have every word or phrase captured in your spreadsheet before you stop working. At this point, you can erase the whiteboard if you must, but I like leaving it up until the next work session. There's something about coming back to the whiteboard and picking up exactly where you left off that helps your brain reengage. Not everyone has the luxury of hogging the whiteboard for several days, which is another reason you captured everything in that spreadsheet.

With all your ideas on the whiteboard and captured in the

spreadsheet, you're officially done with day 1. Go have a nice dinner and let your brain relax.

THE SOAK

It's best if you can take at least two whole days away from the NameStorm board to let all the words and phrases roll around in your slow-thinking brain. This time allows your subconscious to make connections between disparate concepts, process different ways words and phrases can be interpreted, and observe how these concepts might manifest themselves in the real world around you.

WHY YOU NEED BOTH BRAINS (AGAIN)

We were naming a new SaaS platform for structural engineers and had come up with over 600 different words and concepts to consider. At the end of NameStorm day one, there was one word that just stuck in my head for some reason. I thought it was because it was my favorite and a clear candidate for the name. We did a four-day Soak on that project, so we had plenty of time to consider all the options. On day 2 of the Soak, I was driving to a meeting with a different client and saw this word in six-foot letters on the side of a freight truck. That word stuck in my head because I'd seen it driving all over town for years, not because it was the best name. It was an aha moment for sure, and I was embarrassed I hadn't made the connection before then. The remaining Soak time allowed my slow-thinking brain to sort through the other concepts and come back to the process with a clearer view and fresh perspective.

During the Soak, you'll probably have a few words or concepts that keep coming to mind. That's a signal; pay attention to it. Make a point to remember—or better, write down—those words or phrases so you can revisit them during NameStorm day two. Other people will experience the same thing and bring their words to NameStorm day two. It's worth discussing them with the team to understand why those words stuck with you. You might not use them in the end, but there's a reason they kept popping up in your thoughts, and that's worth exploring with your team.

NAMESTORM DAY TWO

The second session is focused on—you guessed it—*convergent thinking*. The goal of this session is to distill all these words down to ten or fewer words that will become your Name Candidates. You'll need your giant whiteboard, dry-erase markers, your spreadsheet, some sharpies, and a lot of sticky notes.

At this point, it's helpful to use some software to help keep track of things. You already have your spreadsheet, but you'll want something else to keep things organized as you go through the next steps of the process. We've used mind maps, online whiteboards and sticky note tools, and other collaboration software for this. One tool that works reasonably well is StormBoard (StormBoard.com). It's basically an online whiteboard with sticky notes you can arrange however you like.

Start by looking at your whiteboard (or spreadsheet) and all the concepts you've written down. Get back in the headspace of all the concepts for a few minutes, then you can erase the whiteboard. It's time to dig in.

Go through your spreadsheet and write each word or concept on a sticky note, either real or virtual (you don't need both), and stick them on your whiteboard. Group similar words and concepts by whatever you feel they have in common. Usually, this is by definition or similarity in meaning. Don't eliminate any words yet! This will help you identify clusters of concepts that came out of NameStorm day one and will help the team see a more macrolevel view of how you're thinking about the name. When you're done, you should take a photo of the whiteboard or save a version or screenshot of whichever software you're using. It helps if you can print it out in large format to use as a reference later.

UNDERSTANDING WORD CHARACTER

Next, you'll want to arrange the words on the Word Character Matrix, which arranges words on a spectrum of *Literal* to *Abstract* on one axis and *Soft* to *Sharp* on another axis. This matrix will help you and your team understand how different words can carry different connotations and how they might influence the overall perception of the name.

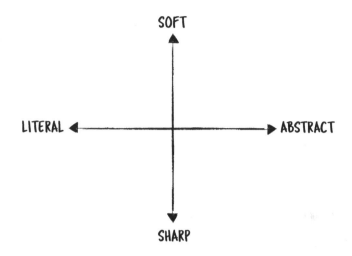

To download a copy of the Word Character Matrix, visit Loopsbook.com/resources.

Consider these words: "kind" is soft and literal, "guru" is soft and abstract, "confidence" is literal and abstract, and "laser" is sharp and literal. You get the idea.

Some of the words might be difficult to place, especially ones like our AltiTech example. Work with your team to place them in a spot on the matrix that the majority of you can agree on. After you have all the words placed on the Word Character Matrix, save it for reference, again, printing it out if you can.

With all your words and these two assets in hand, it's time

to start exploring the words and eliminating things that don't resonate with the group. By this time, a few favorites will be emerging. That's fine, but it's still too early to make any final judgments. Let's move to the next step.

IT'S TAXONOMY TIME

Remember the Name Taxonomy we did a few pages back? The one where we looked at the names of all the competing brands and products in our ecosystem? Now it's time to look at that again and see how our list of names might fit. You don't have to put all our words on the taxonomy, especially since a lot of them just don't make sense for our brand. What we do need to understand is where the gaps are in the marketplace.

Are there a lot of names in any one type? Oftentimes we'll see clusters of names in one or two areas of the taxonomy. Maybe there are a lot of companies with invented names (common with tech startups) or a cluster of functional names (common with professional services firms). Look for an area where there aren't a lot of competing names and think about which words on your spreadsheet might fit there.

Sometimes your market might not respond well to names outside of their comfort zone. Professional accountants, for example, might not be comfortable with a product named "LazerTax" (intentionally misspelled) because it's too edgy or risky for them. Always consider what will resonate with your target market over where you might see a gap in the taxonomy.

ELIMINATION ROUNDS

Now you should have your Similarity Groupings, Name Character Matrix, and Name Taxonomy all in front of you and available for reference. It's time to start removing the ones that don't make sense.

First, add a column to your spreadsheet to track whether a name has been eliminated. This will help you track and sort the names later. Then go through the names on your spreadsheet in any order you like and discuss each of them with your team. Ask, "Does it feel right for the brand?" A lot of them will be easy to eliminate, so just mark them on the spreadsheet and move on. **Do not delete them!** You'll want to keep all the things you discussed and removed because, inevitably, someone will propose an idea, thinking it's new, only to find it's something the team already eliminated. Don't judge them for it. This always happens because the human brain just can't keep all the possible words and combinations in memory.

As you go through the list, you'll probably eliminate most

of the words, leaving a few dozen for further discussion. Once you're down to a dozen or so, it's time to start really comparing the survivors to see which ones go to the final round. These are your finalists.

NAME SCORING

Now that you have a dozen or so names you can live with, it's time to score them using these criteria:

- **Appearance:** How does the name look? Is it easy to spell? When you look at it, do you understand it?
- **Distinctiveness:** Does the name stand out? Does it have depth? Is there meaning behind it?
- **Humanity:** Things that are scientific and technical don't seem to be very human. Things that are cold and analytical don't seem very human.
- **Mouthfeel:** Fun to say, right? That's the point. Is it fun to say the name? It's more fun to say Mailchimp than ConstantContact.
- **Trademark:** Can you defend the intellectual property? Is there another company already using that name, or a confusingly similar one? Is there another company using the domain name?

Pro Tip: The US Patent and Trade office has a database called TESS which holds all the registered trademarks for the United States. Do a search of the TESS database to see if there are any trademark conflicts. Also, always consult with an intellectual property attorney to verify you're in the clear with a new name. Lawsuits aren't cheap, so avoid one if you can.

DOMAIN NAME AND SOCIAL MEDIA AVAILABILITY

As you go through scoring the names, you'll want to check domain name availability. We always check .com, .net, .org, .co, and .us; and depending on the name, we'll check other Top Level Domains (or TLDs) where it makes sense. For example, if the name ends with the letters "es," we'll check the Spanish TLD, .es. If the name ends in "ly," we'll check the Libyan TLD .ly. You get the idea. There are literally hundreds of TLDs, so check with your favorite domain name registrar to see what's available for your name.

As you might imagine, all the common words are taken, so you might need to mix things up to get a name that's available. Sometimes we'll add a prefix or suffix that makes sense. If you're building an app, you can add "app" to the name, like *AltiTechApp.com* or *@AltiTechApp*. Or you can prefix it with "Use" to get *UseAltiTech.com* and *@UseAltiTech*. You can also use an underscore, hyphen, or other creative punctuation to get the handle you want. These names might not be ideal, but they will get the job done for now.

Domain name and social media handle availability should factor highly into your scoring. Websites like InstantDomainSearch.com and Namechk.com can speed up this process. If you can't get a domain with your name in it, it will be much harder to build a brand.

HANDLING SQUATTERS

Lots of domains and social media handles are taken but aren't being used. You should note that in your spreadsheet. It doesn't hurt to reach out to whoever owns the domain or handle and ask if they're willing to sell it. Some social media platforms don't allow the sale of handles in their Terms of Service, so check with them before doing anything that violates those terms.

For domain names, you can usually contact the current owner through the domain registrar or by doing a "Whois" search at *whois.icann.org*.

THE SCORING PROCESS

Create a new sheet in your spreadsheet with the finalist names one per row, and each of the categories above in columns. Then, one by one, score each name on each criterion with your team.

The name with the highest score isn't always your winner,

but it is an indicator of the strongest competitor. It's okay if you still have several candidates. It's time for another Soak—a week this time—to give your slow brain time to do its work. When you get back together with your team and discuss which names bubbled up for everybody, usually one or two names will emerge. Keep discussing with your team until you reach a consensus. It might take a while, and that's okay. Use these questions to spur discussion:

- Which will be the easiest for our target market to remember?
- Which is the most distinctive amongst our competition?
- Which feels the most aligned with our Brand Ethos?
- Which will be the easiest to defend in the market, from an IP perspective?
- Which is the most fun to say?
- Feel free to add your own questions and discuss as much as you need. This is a very important step in the process, but remember, it isn't final and forever. Plenty of companies and products have launched under a less than ideal name and rebranded after they gained enough customers to stand on their own. That said, you want something that's durable, something you and the team can live with for the foreseeable future, and most importantly, something your customers can relate to and remember.

I mentioned earlier coming up with a name for a product that helps buildings keep from swaying in powerful winds. That's an actual client we helped through this process. They settled on the name Hummingbird Kinetics. Their industry is very engineering heavy, with a lot of companies that have functional names, but nothing evocative or descriptive.

As we bounced around ideas, we kept coming back to the idea of stability. A hummingbird is stable, regardless of what is going on around it. The wings are going, but the body stays still as the hummingbird does its work. However, "hummingbird" isn't defensible by IP. We needed "Kinetics" to tie the name to their engineering audience and defend the IP. By using an evocative name, Hummingbird Kinetics stood apart from its competition.

CREATING BRAND STANDARDS: LOGOS, COLORS, TYPOGRAPHY, AND USAGE GUIDELINES

Now that you have a name, the next logical step is creating a logo, picking colors, and building out your brand standards. The basics you'll need:

- A logo that looks good in two colors (usually black and white), at small sizes (like an app icon), and at large sizes (like T-shirts and print materials)
- A color palette with one primary color, two secondary colors, and a few shades of gray
- A font for your product or company name (when it appears as or next to your logo)
- Fonts for your website and marketing materials, usually one font for the headlines and one font for the body copy. And yes, they should be different from the one you use for your name.
- A document that describes how your logo, colors, and fonts can and cannot be used. For example, you shouldn't put the light color logo on top of a light colored background, don't stretch or distort the logo, and so on.

Creating all these assets is an important step in the process and one that takes a significant amount of artistic help (or a significant amount of luck). Logos can be cheap or very expensive. There's no direct relation between how much you spend and how good your logo is, but it's safe to say spending a little to get a quality product is generally worth the investment. Think of it this way: if you take the cost of a professionally designed logo and divide it by the number of times people will see it over its lifetime, you quickly realize it's worth the investment to get it right.

That said, the amount of effort you should put into it depends on a few factors: your budget, the creative abilities of your team, how much time you have to invest, and whether you have to comply with any existing brand standards. How much of your time and money you choose to invest is up to you. Here are a few thoughts that might help you decide.

FOR EXISTING COMPANIES

You probably already have some sort of company branding you need to comply with. If that's the case, you probably don't need to think about creating logos or other branding assets. Feel free to go talk to your marketing team and skip to the next chapter if you want.

FOR STARTUPS

The honest truth for most startups is until you've proven people like your product, you really shouldn't invest too much in a logo and color palette. This might seem counterintuitive at first, but your logo can evolve just like your product evolves. It doesn't need to be perfect from the first day.

The quick and dirty way to get something that works until you have traction and need to refine or even rethink your logo is to use a website like 99designs, Upwork, Fiverr, or DesignCrowd. Any of them will be able to deliver a full brand package for a few hundred bucks. It won't be great, but it will serve its purpose.

- **The upside:** You'll get a logo and brand standards done pretty quickly and with minimal effort on your part.
- **The downside:** You won't have as much control over the process, and you'll probably get something that isn't super unique.

HIRING A PROFESSIONAL BRAND DESIGNER

There are lots of agencies capable of building a great brand package for you. Whether you find a local agency or work with someone remote or online, I suggest you get them to send you an outline of their process, timelines, and budget in advance. Any agency that doesn't have a solid process for developing a brand package should be avoided.

THERE'S A LOT MORE, BUT LET'S STAY FOCUSED

Brand development is a complex, nuanced, and highly subjective art. You can spend a lot of time and energy on it, and if you're not careful, you can fall into a rabbit hole of color, typography, and other details that might not be the best use of your time at this phase of the product.

Since this book is primarily about building products, we'll skip the rest of the details. If you're interested, there's a full whitepaper available at Loopsbook.com/branding that outlines the entire process.

HOW FREDDIE KEEPS MAILCHIMP HUMAN

All brands evolve over time. Early on, Mailchimp's logo was a clip-art-styled monkey's face wearing a hat. Then in 2006, based on customer feedback, they decided to change it to just a wordmark. In 2008 they decided it was time to bring the chimp back, and they hired a renowned visual designer to make it happen. Today they have a very clean and professional visual brand that is a reflection of their brand personality.

2001

2005

2008

2018

Your brand will evolve just like your product does. It's easy to look at big-name brands and think you have to match their quality or perception. You can't.

You shouldn't compare your work in progress to their finished product.

Too many people get caught up in trying to make their logo perfect and forget that, just like the product they are building, the logo can change as the business grows. It's just as important not to get caught up in overthinking the perfect brand execution as it is not to get caught up in the perfect product execution. Let your brand have its own Loops. You'll be happier that way.

Chapter Six

STEP FIVE: BUILDING AT SPEED

"Build half a product, not a half-assed product."

JASON FRIED, CO-FOUNDER AND CEO, BASECAMP

Mailchimp prides itself on building delight into the user interface of its web app. Early versions of the web app included fun little touches. For example, when you clicked the company's "Freddie" logo in the header, a funny quote would appear. Every time you clicked the logo, it would change what Freddie said. Sometimes he would tell a dumb joke. Sometimes he would tell you how great you looked. Sometimes he'd let you know you were doing a great job. Friendly, encouraging words to add some delight to the interface.

It was a tiny bit of polish, like adding a dash of finishing salt to a dish you've cooked. These sayings added a nice human touch to elevate the experience Mailchimp's customers had using the app.

Another thing Mailchimp did early on was hire talented people who understood the brand and product objectives very well. These people helped Mailchimp stay focused on customer needs and delivering value. They could have looked only at metrics like sign-ups and revenue, but what they cared about from the start was task completion and customer satisfaction. One way they measured task completion was by looking at how many emails were successfully sent and how many emails stayed in draft status. If a lot of people created drafts they never sent, it would be an indication that the tool might be too hard to use. Nobody would be satisfied with a tool that's too hard to use. The product team would reach out to people who didn't complete the task of sending an email and ask what happened. This feedback helped them understand customers better and improve the product.

To this day, Mailchimp talks to their customers relentlessly. Top executives go on personal one-on-one visits with their customers, and not just the customers who pay a lot of money as you might guess. Mailchimp executives will fly to a small city and visit a mom-and-pop retail shop who pay $79 a month to discuss how the owners are using email marketing. By understanding and solving the problems those users experience, they can use what they learn to solve problems for other customers.

That's why the first three Loops in this process are so important. You never stop doing research, you never stop developing prototypes, and you never stop testing and tweaking your ideas. These steps are essential, and to drive product innovation, you'll continue to loop back and forth between these steps for as long as you're in business. In the last chapter, we added another Loop— your brand. Now you're ready to build a product to take to market.

YOU'RE NOT BUILDING AN MVP

Before we get into the logistics of building a product and going through iterations with it, I want to reframe your thinking a little. A popular term in the startup world is MVP, or Minimum Viable Product. An MVP is the simplest version of your product that's capable of demonstrating the value you have to offer the customer. A common mistake people make with an MVP is to build something that's too focused on the mechanics of the task. It might help people accomplish the task, but it's not easy to use, and it doesn't generate delight. Consider the illustration below:

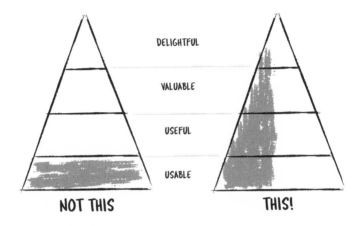

Most people think the MVP just needs to be *viable*. They ask themselves: "Does it prove people can accomplish a task?" They don't think about making it useful, usable, or delightful. They think it's okay to add usability and delight later on. You can do it that way, and people have, but there's a better way.

The best MVPs deliver value on all four levels from the start. Sure, they deliver the raw utility of accomplishing a task. They also do it in a way that's easy and intuitive for the user, and they add a little bit of delight in the process. Brian Chesky and Joe Gebbia, two of the co-founders of Airbnb, said when they first thought about the level of service they wanted to provide, they asked themselves, "How do we take it to 11?" In other words, how can we create an experience that really dazzles the user? What would make the experience so good the customer *wants* to do it again?

What would you rather someone say about what you're building?

- "I used this app and it worked."
- "I used this app and it was awesome!"

You need to start with a sliver of viability, usefulness, usability, and delightfulness, and as you iterate and improve on the product, you want to build sideways across the pyramid to add more of each attribute with each update.

THE MINIMUM DELIGHTFUL PRODUCT

In this chapter, we'll look at building an MDP: Minimum Delightful Product. What is the smallest thing you can build that not only helps someone accomplish a task and generate value but is also fun to use, something that brings a bit of joy into their world?

Delight helps people build an emotional connection to your product. As we all know, people are automatically attracted to products they enjoy using, even if they lack features they might want. Any time you can build a product that is more *enjoyable* than your competitor's product, you'll have the advantage.

The Zappos mobile app shows us a small way to add delight. When a Zappos VIP logs into the app, it rains VIP badges from the top of the screen. Totally unnecessary. A little silly if you think about it, but it adds a tiny bit of delight to the experience. Another example is when you add an item to your cart, you'll see an animation of a cat wearing a parachute with a box that falls into the cart icon and updates the quantity of items in the cart. They could have easily just added to the number on the cart icon, but they chose to add a little bit of delight. Ask yourself, how can you add delight to your product? Where are the tiny opportunities to make something that will put a smile on the users' faces? Take those opportunities when you can. They might feel silly now, but those little differences add up to create a memorable experience. That said, don't overdo it. Too many little things aimed at adding delight can be too much and feel like a cheap gimmick instead of an enhancement to the experience.

AS THIN AS POSSIBLE

In this age of technology it's really easy to think about building a piece of software to solve almost any problem. The "there's an app for that" mentality is pervasive. What most people don't realize is exactly how expensive software can be to build. The good news is you don't have to build software right away in many cases. A lot of what products and services do behind the scenes can be delivered manually by a human being. In the early stages of product development, I'm giving you permission to cheat. You can create *manuware*, which is a term I just invented to describe creating a product that might *look* like software but is actually powered by manual labor behind the scenes. (Remember the Adaptly story?)

I recommend starting this way because it's cheaper, faster, and will teach you a lot. It may not seem cheaper because you or someone on your team will have to do a lot of manual labor. But putting in all that manual labor will tell you what works and what doesn't work, and what repeated processes make sense to be replaced with code. When you go to build your first piece of software, you'll have a clearer target to hit, which lowers your risk and saves you money.

Of course, there are some types of products and services where you can't do things manually because they're predicated on the underlying technology itself, like a complex data analysts or a machine learning algorithm. Obviously, that's a bit different. However, even in those instances, you don't have to build a lot of surrounding software to deliver the core value of the product. In the beginning, your goal should be to simply deliver an MDP to your customers, not a fully finished one. After all, software is never finished. Never.

MANUAL RANKINGS

Another example is a music streaming platform we worked with that updated all their "Most Popular" lists manually in early versions of the app. Sure, they could have written a little code to do it automatically. That might have actually been faster. But the process of manually looking at play counts and updating the list helped them understand how to spot when people were using bots to falsely inflate their play counts. This was important since it helped make sure the Most Popular lists were accurate and not prone to manipulation by bots and other bad actors trying to game the system. That helped artists and fans gain confidence in the numbers, and built loyalty to the platform. Sometimes the hard way is the best way.

PROOF OF CONCEPT

Another term you'll hear often in the startup world is *Proof of Concept*, or POC. This is a super lightweight app you create to prove a solution and its critical point of value. You might have developed a POC in step 3 if you did more advanced wireframing, and if so, it's time to turn that POC into an MDP. Keep in mind that sometimes this doesn't unfold the way you think it will. Let me give you two examples.

WATER QUALITY CHECK

A company came to us wanting to build a platform for people to get information about water quality in their neighborhood. They had this idea for an elaborate website with maps where users could browse their neighborhood or put in their address or zip code and look up detailed water quality data for their area. If the water in their area was high in chlorine, for example, they would see details on chlorine and other chemical levels, links to research about effects of chlorine in drinking water, and links to buy chlorine-specific water filters. The problem was they hadn't proven that people cared about finding out the water quality in their neighborhood, so a big website seemed risky.

We recommended a text message service where users could text their zip code to a number and get a response with the water quality in their area. If their area had high chlorine, they'd be sent a list of chlorine filters with links to purchase them on Amazon through an affiliate program.

With the text message service, they didn't have to think about managing products or writing a lot of code. This was the proof of concept they needed. With a tiny bit of code, they're already generating revenue instead of spending time and money building a web platform.

PTSD COMMUNITY

Another company we worked with wanted to build a platform to connect people with PTSD to other people with

PTSD so they could support one another. It's proven that people with PTSD are greatly helped by being able to talk about it with someone who understands, so this seemed like a great and noble cause.

This client wanted to build elaborate web and mobile apps with a marketplace, user profiles, and lots of helpful content. That's a heavy lift. All they really needed to prove value to users was connect two people. So we built a text message chatbot instead. Users could text a number to ask to speak to someone in their area, and after providing a few details, they'd get matched up. This enabled the client to focus on figuring out the mechanics of matching people based on location and personality, and not spend all their effort building software.

Once this client proved their solution connected people consistently and these people were having meaningful conversations with others, then their team could go out and build a product that was focused on making those interactions easier and more effective.

GETTING TO THE NEXT LEVEL

Let's say you started off with the *manuware* approach to prove you can deliver value to your customers. You've seen some success, and a few people are paying for your product. The Proof of Concept is working!

Now you need to think about how to build on that success and continue to design, develop, and ship small enhancements that create more value for your users. There are a lot of decisions to make. You might have made some of them already. You need to choose a tech stack (all the technology you'll use to create and manage the product), create a Design System, define how to use your prototypes to guide development, how to get code into production, how to test and measure performance of the product, and a lot more.

Honestly, by this time, you probably already have decided—or at least have strong opinions about—which tech stack you'll use. Great. Nothing in this book is intended to sway you towards one technology or another. I want you to think about how to get the most from your technology, and when I say, "the most," I mean the most value for your customers.

DESIGN OPERATIONS

As my good friend Jared Spool says, "Design is the rendering of intent." It's the process of getting ideas out of your head and into the real world. Building on that thought, Design Operations is how you define and manage the process of getting ideas out of your head and into the real world.

In simple terms, Design Operations are the processes,

tasks, activities, and behaviors it takes to create a product. It's a lot of what we've already covered in this book, and it's how your team works together to make it all happen. It's more than a script you follow or a specific set of tools. It's all of that bundled together. It's partly things you do and partly how you think about the things you do.

The typical company has three primary roles, or types of people: Visionaries, Technicians, and Operators. In a startup, the Visionary is usually the founder who had the idea in the first place. In larger companies, the Visionary usually comes from a business team and is someone who is trying to achieve a strategic goal for the organization. They are typically goal-oriented thinkers with a bias for action. Technicians are usually developers, engineers, and analysts—the people who think logically, want order, and avoid chaos. Operators are the people who make sure things are getting done. They are typically relationship-oriented and help manage the tension and build consensus between the contrasting forces of Visionaries and Technicians.

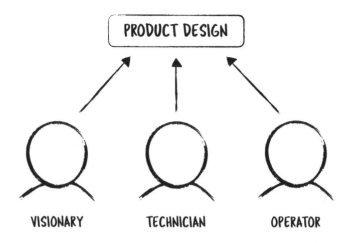

VISIONARY   TECHNICIAN   OPERATOR

All three roles are essential. You might fill all three roles, or you might have different people in each one. That's not important for this conversation. What is important is that you have a common language for all of these types of people (or roles) to refer to as they are building the product together.

THE DESIGN SYSTEM

This common definition of how things look and work is called a Design System. It can be seen as an extension of your Brand Standards, and it certainly uses those standards at its core, but it's so much more than that. A Design System includes all the different types of assets, artifacts, patterns, and guidance on how to use it all. Inside the Design System are all the buttons, navigation elements, form fields, images, icons, and everything you need to build an interface. It's an essential resource to help guide product development and make sure everyone stays on the same page.

Think about the apps on your phone; they all have a slightly different look and feel. They might use buttons in a slightly different way, but every app has some type of button. Every app has to display content of some type, and most apps have a way for you to enter information, even if it's just your name and email address to sign up. Every interface you use has these basic building blocks. You'll need to define how all these building blocks look in your product. A Design System helps define and document how all these things look in one single source of truth, which leads to consistency through the entire interface.

The Design System also dictates how interface elements behave when someone uses them. Do you tap a button or swipe the screen? Do things change shape or color when you tap them? Does it move? Does it wiggle? These are a few examples of little behaviors (or microinteractions) you want to define in the Design System so everyone knows how things should look and behave.

Another part of the Design System is the language you use, typically called "Voice and Tone." For example, "click here" is an action. But more accurately, "send email" is a direct action related to a workflow. Thinking back to your Brand Ethos: How would your brand say something to a user? That should guide your Voice and Tone. It wouldn't make any sense to have an edgy brand with a dull corporate-sounding Voice and Tone, now would it?

Here's the truth: developers typically don't care what color a button is or how big it is, they just want to make sure the thing works from a technical perspective. The user interface (UI) and user experience (UX) designers, on the other hand, do care how big the button is and what color it is. They also want to make sure the thing works from the user's perspective.

Both groups share a common interest in making sure things work. Where their interests vary is in the appearance of something versus the accuracy and efficiency of the code that's powering it. So we need to use the Design System as the common language.

The Design System is a single source of truth for how things look and work.

ENTER ATOMIC DESIGN

Most of us understand basic biology. You have molecules, atoms, and organisms—the building blocks of life. Atomic

Design is the same concept: it's the building blocks of an application. Brad Frost pioneered the concept of Atomic Design many years ago. I find it's a great way to get everyone understanding how all the different parts of an interface and application come together to make a product. Here's how it works.

An atom is the smallest possible component. It can't be broken down any further. A button is a good example of an atom.

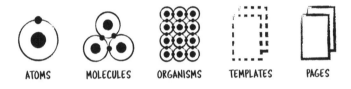

ATOMS　　MOLECULES　　ORGANISMS　　TEMPLATES　　PAGES

Molecules are groups of atoms that serve a certain purpose. A call to action or a bio card with someone's photo are good examples of molecules.

An organism is a collection of molecules that performs a larger function. A navigation bar is a good example of an organism. The navigation bar might have a logo, dropdown menus, a login form, and a search box. All of those things are atoms or molecules coming together to make an organism.

When you design a system, define as many of the atoms, molecules, and organisms as you can. You may not know what all your organisms will be yet, but you can start with atoms and molecules—the building blocks—and go from there. Later on, you'll build templates for pages once you understand what needs to be on the screen at each point in the workflow. Designers and developers can work together to figure out what needs to happen. A UX designer can come in to make sure everything is working together.

For a list of Design System tools, check out Loopsbook. com/resources.

If we've created all of our buttons, form fields, navigation tools, and everything else, we enable the developer (who isn't concerned about aesthetics) to go and get the exact attributes and parameters they need in order to build something that's compliant with the Design System. It enables everyone on the team to look at the application and know immediately whether or not it complies with the standards. They can easily see that this button is green, but our standard is blue. That will lead to discussions of consistency.

Another wonderful thing about Design Systems is they are adaptable. If you decide to change the color blue you are using for buttons (maybe you want to make it a bit lighter), someone on the visual design team can make that change, commit it to the Design System, and the next time the software is built, that color blue automatically populates throughout the entire application. The Design System is the source of truth.

A PRACTICAL NOTE

I mentioned Atomic Design is a great way to think about the different parts of an interface and how you use them to build a product. This method of breaking down an interface into its smallest common components is a great way to get your team thinking about how everything will fit together, and to help illustrate the importance of consistency across the entire system. However, in practice, the line between an atom and a molecule gets blurry pretty fast. Don't be super concerned with every little piece of the Design System fitting neatly into one of those categories. When the team is working to crank out the next release, they'll be thinking about buttons, groups of form fields, and pretty much any other part of the system as *components*, not whether it's an atom or a molecule. So don't get hung up on the semantics.

With your new understanding of Design Operations, you have the first half of the picture of how products get made. Now we're going to dig in to the back half, Development Operations, or DevOps.

DEVELOPMENT OPERATIONS

In parallel to the Design System, you need coding standards—a process for writing code, sharing code, and getting code from a developer's computer to a test environment, where it can be used and tested by the rest of the team, and eventually into Production, where it can be used by your customers. This process is called development operations, or DevOps.

Most people will tell you that DevOps is separate from design. While that can be true, that's not necessarily the best practice. DevOps is a critical component of Design Operations because you can make things look pretty all day long, but it doesn't matter if you can't ship to Production.

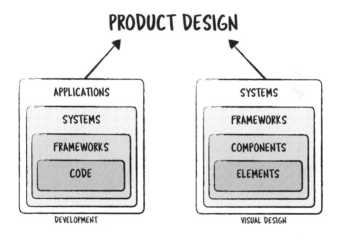

THE TECH STACK

Before you can decide which technology to use, you need to think about where your product will be used. Is this a mobile app? A web app? Something for a certain type of tablet? Think about the context in which your customers will use the application because that's going to inform the technology decisions you make next. Think about Lyft or Instagram. There is not much of a website interface for those products because they were intended to only work with your phone. Airbnb, on the other hand, can be used on any device.

Deciding how and where people are going to use the product helps you understand how you need to build it. If it's just a simple website, you can probably get away with one unified set of code, or codebase, for everything in the beginning. You can always separate things out later as you grow and the product becomes more complex.

With Lyft, for example, at least three codebases are needed: one for iPhones, one for Android, and one common set of code that runs behind the scenes somewhere to match drivers to passengers, process payments, and more. In reality, there are probably many different codebases behind the scenes at Lyft. For the sake of this example, we'll keep it simple.

If you're building an app like Airbnb, you'll have an

iPhone app, an Android app (which are basically wrappers for the web services), and you'll have a separate codebase which runs the website. Then you'll have a backend infrastructure that runs the web services the website and each of the mobile devices connect to for all the core functionality your company provides.

DO YOU REALLY NEED A MOBILE APP?

If you're building something that requires access to device hardware like the camera or the GPS on a phone, that means you need a native app that runs directly on the phone. If you don't need direct access to the device hardware, you can probably get away with building your product on the web and creating a mobile wrapper, or an app that still installs like any other mobile app and simply loads a mobile-optimized version of the website product.

There are also multiple platforms and frameworks that will allow you to write one common codebase which will run on a variety of devices. These "write once, run anywhere" frameworks are great for starting out and getting your app into the hands of customers early on, but they rapidly start to fall short as the complexity of your product grows.

These might be good options if you're still in the MDP or POC phase. Have an honest conversation with your team about your capabilities and the minimal requirements of your app, and make the decision that's right for you.

Once you've made a decision on your tech stack, you have to start writing, testing, and shipping code. This is the part where the nerds start to get excited and where things start to really get real.

WRITING CODE

This book is not about how to write great code. There are countless books and blogs that do a much better job showing you how to write great code than I ever could. I will say there are a few things everyone should know about writing code, and knowing them will help your teams create better products.

VERSION CONTROL

Perhaps the most important thing a software team can do is use a great version control system. I have a strong preference for Git and GitHub, but there are plenty of other systems available. Find the flavor that works for you.

The core concept of version control is that it allows people to work on software together and keep track of their changes, when they were made, and (most importantly) why they were made. If one person writes code to add a feature, the rest of the team can easily see that code, merge it into what they've written, test it, tweak it, and commit it back for everyone else to use.

The concept of branching is critical to version control. A branch is essentially a copy of the master codebase that will be used to create a minor enhancement or fix a bug. When the code changes are made, the branch can be merged back into the master codebase and shipped to production. With version control, you can easily see all the branches, what they were for, and what code was added, changed, or deleted. This makes it very easy to track changes over the history of the codebase.

Version control also makes it easy to look back at changes to your code and see what happened. Want to know why something was changed? Just go back to that point in history and read the comments.

A note about comments: You want your team to write comments about why they wrote the code that way. Not what they wrote but why they wrote it. Why was this the decision they made? What informed the decision? Comments should be written to inform (or remind) someone in the future of why this was done in the past.

Another great reason to use version control is it makes it really easy to revert back to the last working version of something. You want developers to try new things without risk. Having a safety net that makes it easy to recover from failed experiments is a great asset and will empower developers to be more creative when writing code.

A final reason to use version control is that it provides an instant and always current backup to your entire product. It's not a big deal if someone's computer dies because the code is in several other places.

FEATURE FLAGS

One of the more interesting concepts in software design is feature flags. In simple terms, it's wrapping a feature in a simple switch you can turn on and off at any time without writing more code. Think of it like a light switch for a feature, but one you can turn on and off based on who is in the room. With feature flags, you can turn features on for groups of people based on demographics, behavior, time of day, or some combination of each.

Here's an example: Remember our taco delivery app? Let's say we want to allow people in the 30309 zip code to see free fifteen-minute delivery, but for everyone else, delivery costs $2.95 and takes thirty minutes. With a feature flag, we can turn on the fifteen-minute delivery option only for people in that immediate area.

I'm sure you can imagine all the other things you could do with feature flags. They are a powerful way to control which features or functionality you provide to your users.

So now that you've decided on your architecture, have written some code (maybe with a few feature flags), and have version control in place to manage it. How do you get the product into the hands of customers? You have to "ship it."

SHIPPING WITH CONTINUOUS INTEGRATION AND DELIVERY

The concept of Continuous Integration/Continuous Delivery, or "CI/CD," is that a team can make small iterative improvements to a product and get them into the hands of users quickly, efficiently, and with minimal risk.

Without getting into the weeds of development methodologies, let's say you want to improve the way the navigation works in your app. A developer should be able to create a branch of your codebase, write the code needed for the improvement, test it, and if the tests pass, ship it to production without interrupting or jeopardizing the work of anyone else on the team.

A typical process will involve several "environments" where your code can run. These environments are usually Development, Test, Staging, and Production. Production is the public system where customers use the product. Staging is where the team puts changes that are ready to go live and where the final set of tests are run before being "promoted" to Production. Test is typically available to multiple people on the team to access and test the code a developer has written before it is promoted to Staging. Development is usually a developer's own computer, where they can write code and perform simple tests to make sure it does what they expect it to.

A Continuous Integration and Delivery process manages all of this. There is usually a set of automated tests at each step that makes sure the code doesn't fail. What these tests look for and how they do it is up to the team. It's a very detailed and wide-ranging aspect of software development, and I won't go into more detail in this book. What's important is you have some standardized process for ensuring the code that makes it into Production is as performant and bug-free as possible.

BRINGING IT ALL TOGETHER

Think about the apps on your phone being updated and take Amazon as an example. Like many big companies, Amazon changes both their website and their app multiple times per day. They are constantly changing things based on different user needs. Users might not see that change because it's something small. It might be a different shade of blue or a slightly larger typeface, or it might be something intended to influence how people use the app. You might get a slightly different experience with Amazon than other users depending on your age, geography, or the types of products you buy.

Amazon has developed a process for deciding what goes into their apps, and it's similar to all the things you've read about in this book. It's an idea meritocracy where they use experiments and data to drive decisions. Let's see how it all fits together with a hypothetical situation. For example, they might have the following goal:

We want to increase discovery of Alexa skills on Amazon.com by 5 percent.

Going back to Chapter 2, they do research to understand what types of things could help drive discovery of Alexa skills. Obviously, changing the entire homepage of Amazon.com to talk about Alexa skills would do it, though I doubt that idea would fly with the rest of the business units.

Instead of blindly trying things and potentially making big mistakes, they talk to other teams and stakeholders within Amazon and review previous research on how other similar goals have been met in the past. They ask, "How might we?" and through divergent and convergent sessions come up with a hypothesis:

If we change the navigation so that the Alexa skills marketplace is more prominent, we will see a 5 percent increase in the people using Alexa skills.

They take this hypothesis to the design team for the next step. The design team comes up with a few ideas for what "more prominent" means and creates experiments they can use to test which option yields the best results. Let's say they want to test three options:

1. Moving "Alexa Skills" to the third position in the navigation.
2. Leave the text "Alexa Skills" in the same location but make the text larger.
3. Leave the text "Alexa Skills" in the same location but make it look like a button instead of plain text.

Then they create prototypes for each of the options which show the development team how to change the interface. From there, the developers create branches of the codebase for each of the experiments and make the changes needed to comply with the prototypes. They wrap each feature in a feature flag to make it easier to run the experiments and begin to promote the code up to Production. Assuming all the tests pass, the code makes it into Production, and the business team can begin to run the experiments.

Amazon is known for turning on features for small groups of people for very short amounts of time. They have so much traffic that they can get enough data in thirty seconds to analyze whether a hypothesis worked. At a startup scale, you'll need to leave features on longer and test with a wider array of people.

If the hypothesis was proven to be true and did not have a negative impact on any other important business metrics, then, using feature flags, they can turn that feature on for a larger group of people. They might start by making the feature available to 10 percent of people in a specific zip code, then increase it to 20 percent, then 40 percent, and so on to slowly roll out features while ensuring that they work and can scale.

If you are small-scale right now, you want to put these processes in place now. The software you write has to fundamentally shift at a very rapid, iterative pace, and you'll want to develop good discipline around that. By doing so, you'll be able to respond to market change, fix bugs, and release new updates faster as you grow.

BUT I'M NOT A TECHNICAL PERSON!

You need a great team to build the product you have in mind. You'll need user interface designers, visual designers, and interaction designers. You need people who can understand the workflows and make sure appropriate information is on the screen at the right time in that workflow. You're going to need people who understand how to publish code and get it live on servers in the cloud. You need people with more skill than you are probably ready to hire, so it's great to find an agency or a development partner that can help you find the people you need.

You might be able to find a co-founder who can help you do a lot of the technical work, but chances are there are going to be a lot of questions that you can't answer on your own, and it's best to get involved with an experienced product design agency or some other support network that can help you make those decisions the right way.

Some of the full-service companies use a cookie-cutter process that is highly templated. Starting out, that might be okay. Remember, your main focus isn't about the visual right now; your main focus is about proving value to your customer. Another option is to hire a consulting company to advise you and provide access to their network of product design talent.

In addition to full product strategy, consulting, and design services, one of the things my company offers is a service where I come on board your team as fractional Chief Product Officer. When you hire me, you also get access to my team and my network of talent. I'm not selling you on my services. There are other people who do the same thing, so shop around. Look for tech incubators, meetups, and other community events and resources. Talk to people doing the things you need done and see what resources are available near you. You might be surprised at what you find.

THE POWER OF AN ADVISORY COUNCIL

As long as you're continuously talking to your customers,

you don't necessarily have to add more features, but you do need to improve how well you're solving their problems. A great way to do this early on is by forming an advisory council.

Identify your best and most important customers; they should be people who can help shape the future of the product. In B2B software, this might be your biggest customers. Or maybe they're customers in a certain market where you want to grow. Think about your most strategically valuable customers and invite them into the product development process. Their input will be invaluable in guiding product decisions and development. They will love being a part of the process, and it won't cost you a dime.

These people should become involved in the development of the product. By giving them early access, they get a hint of what you're thinking, building, and testing. You're building trust with them and helping them feel special. When someone feels like they get special treatment, they are going to give you something in return—in this case, valuable information.

Remember, these people should be your best customers, but "best" is strategically defined. It may not be the customer who pays the most. What you're looking for are customers who contribute what you need to know to the conversation. If 10 percent of your customers are in Europe and you're looking to expand there, it doesn't matter if that 10 percent of customers provides a small fraction of your revenue. If they have information you can use to develop the roadmap to get to Europe, invite them to join your advisory council.

An advisory council member is *not* the customer who complains the most or the loudest. Some people will buy a product because they think it does something they want only to find out the software doesn't do that. Instead of going and finding a different product, they will pound you with suggestions to make it do what they want. Customer feedback is valuable, but sometimes customers are just using the wrong product.

Of course, there are always exceptions. When PayPal was getting started, they had a support email address they didn't even check for over a year. They knew the problem they were trying to solve, and if they opened that inbox, they'd risk getting distracted by other problems and not reaching their goals.

Throughout this book, I've told you to listen to your customer, and that's still true. But you also have to be careful not to get pulled off course and fall into solving someone else's problem. If you've done enough research, you should have enough confidence in the problem you are solving and enough clarity to stay focused.

Of course your product should evolve and grow. Trying to meet the changing needs of your customers, responding to market shifts, and dealing with competitors is a bit like trying to hit a moving target. You're never done with the process. Your product is a living, breathing thing. It will require continuous attention and improvement, kind of like parenting. When you have a child, you don't ever stop being a parent, even after your child leaves the house. When your product hits the market, you're still responsible for it, and you always will be.

MAILCHIMP KEPT THE RIGHT FOCUS

One year, around Christmas time, one of Mailchimp's largest revenue-generating customers was experiencing a major technical issue. A junior tech support staffer was working over the holiday, and the customer threatened to cancel if the issue wasn't fixed by a certain date. Well, Mailchimp simply couldn't fix it fast enough. Given the time crunch, it was an impossible ask.

The junior tech support staffer emailed Ben Chestnut, one of the co-founders, to let him know that one of the biggest customers was going to cancel if they couldn't fix the issue. Ben looked at the customer's revenue and compared it to the combined revenue from all their other customers.

This one customer may have been the biggest in terms of

the amount of money coming in, but when Ben looked at the long tail of all the other customers—those paying $20, $40, or $100 per month—the revenue from the big customer wasn't that big of a deal.

Ben's response was: "Let them cancel." He didn't want Mailchimp to be dictated by a few large customers. He wanted the company to solve problems for as many people as possible, so he let that big customer go. Ben wrote about this in a post called "Whale Hunting or Scale Hunting." I suggest you read it (tinyletter.com/ben/letters/whale-hunting-or-scale-hunting).

You can develop a valuable product as long as your customers are happy. There was a risk that making the change demanded by their big customer could've been detrimental to Mailchimp's smaller customers. You have to focus on taking care of the right customers, not just the biggest.

Mailchimp is a private company, so we don't know for a fact, but according to *Forbes*, they are worth over $4 billion. It was started by a few guys with a hunch that if they solved a problem for their customers, they could build a business around that solution.

They were right, and they've grown to be a multibillion-dollar company because they stay focused on the needs of their customer and iterate the product in a way that reflects those changing needs. The product and their brand have evolved over the past decade and will continue to do so. Ironically, Mailchimp recently got back into the postcard business, so you can now send snail mail through an email marketing company.

The irony there is hilarious, but it's just another example of how they've adapted to market trends. They didn't decide to do postcards and then take that product to customers. They got feedback from customers and then built a solution to the problem they saw.

CONCLUSION

"Success is no accident. It is hard work, perseverance, learning, studying, sacrifice and most of all, love of what you are doing or learning to do."

PELÉ

As we've seen, it's best to think about human-centered business design as a series of Loops. There are the smaller Loops in steps 1 through 2 that give you the confidence to move on to steps 4 and 5. Then there's the big Loop between step 5 and the first three steps to ensure that you're constantly innovating your product design.

Will every idea develop into a viable product? Absolutely not. There are a lot of things that can go wrong. The principles and tactics that we have talked about in this book increase your chances of success but do not guarantee anything. Maybe you're trying to solve the wrong problem. Maybe something in the process wasn't done well. Maybe you hired the wrong people, or you wasted time and money building the wrong solutions. Maybe someone else came along and solved the problem better than you did.

There are so many ways that an idea or a company can fail, and you have to remain sober about your odds. Following the steps in this book will increase your odds, but it doesn't make it a sure bet.

There are lots of ideas out there, and lots of people who have ideas. Only a few of those ideas are viable, and of the few that turn into hunches, even fewer will develop into products that launch businesses. Sometimes the market isn't ready yet, or the technology doesn't exist yet, or you don't have the team put together yet, or the solution is just too damn expensive. There are a lot of occasions where something might seem like a brilliant idea, but it just isn't possible now, and it might never be possible. There are brilliant ideas that the market may never pay for. There are all kinds of roadblocks and pitfalls that can derail a product. Remember that potential failure points exist.

The flip side of that, of course, is that success is a very real possibility. And with confidence in your ideas and clarity on how to execute on them, you should pursue that success.

WHAT COMES NEXT?

After you've followed the processes outlined in this book, you might launch a business built around a product that solves a problem for your customers. Maybe you haven't started yet. Maybe you already have a product in market and have customers who are generating revenue. Regardless of where you're starting, hopefully this book has given you tools, tactics, and examples of how to get where you want to be.

One of the biggest parts of building a successful company is the go-to-market strategy. How do you get more customers like the ones you interviewed early on? Are you going to advertise? Are you going to partner with someone? Are you going to put ads on Spotify or Google, or will you do print ads or billboards?

There are a lot of sales and marketing techniques that go into building a go-to market strategy. It's an extremely complex process, and you need support to do that.

You also need to consider general administrative tasks. You need bank accounts, a way to manage your books, to take payments, to do payroll—all the components that make a business work. You need to set up email for the people you work with. You'll need to share documents using something like Dropbox or Google Drive. You need to track all of your expenses and income with an accounting platform like QuickBooks or Xero. You need to pay people, so you'll need payroll and an HR team. It's a ton of work, but working with other business owners can be a great way to get practical tips on how to make sure the business is running smoothly and efficiently.

You've gone from riding a unicycle to a bicycle. The front tire is your product that solves a real problem people have. Now you need to think about the back tire.

The back tire is the business engine that is driving the product forward. That's accounting, legal, HR, infrastructure, and all the other bits and pieces that you need to run a business. There's a lot to think about!

We're not covering that in this book, but there are plenty of resources you can check out. I've compiled some of my favorites at Loopsbook.com/resources.

OUTSIDE HELP

One option for your product is to join an incubator or accelerator program. There are a lot of them out there. Techstars and Y Combinator are two examples. Incubators and accelerator programs are good because they connect you with people who have talent in a number of areas: design, development, legal, accounting, and fundraising, among other areas.

They also give you an essential support ecosystem of other people who are building products. You can bounce ideas off of them or talk through problems.

One program that might help you through the process is our thirty-six-week program, which you can find at 36Weeks.com. This website will give you resources and guide you through the processes outlined in this book on a week-by-week basis.

At this point, if you have a product people are willing to

pay for, you deserve a pat on the back. Congratulations, good luck on your mission, and call me if you need help.

ACKNOWLEDGMENTS

I have to begin by thanking my incredibly supportive and patient wife, Stacey. Without her boundless love and encouragement, my career, and this book with it, would not be possible.

My sincerest thanks to Katie, Michael, Steve, Wells, Cleo, Lacey, Sophia, Jina, Rogie, Miranda, Jennifer, Jacklyn, Jesse, Charlene, Annabel, Sierra, Moses, Keri, Kelly, Snook, Julie, and everyone else from the Nine Labs team for all your hard work and dedication.

Thank you to each and every client we've worked with. You allowed us to help solve your challenges. I'm deeply thankful for your trust and loyalty.

Thanks to Greg Storey, Nick Finck, Ed Reiker, Evan LaPointe, Sean Gerety, and Greg Hoy for helping with early drafts of the book and for their sage advice.

And finally thank you to Josh Raymer, Kayla Sokol, and the rest of the publishing team. You kept me focused and the book is better as a result. It wasn't possible without you.

ABOUT THE AUTHOR

My sophomore and junior year of high school, I was in a punk rock band. We played the Battle of the Bands, but when we showed up to play, the sound system wasn't set up. Instead of waiting around to see what was going to happen, I pushed the sound guy aside and set up the system so we could play. The owner of the venue saw me do that, so he pulled me aside and asked, "Do you know how this sound system works?"

I told him I did. I'd been setting up the sound equipment for our band for a long time, and as a result, I'd developed a fascination with audio technology. The owner asked if I'd be willing to help figure out what was wrong with the club's sound system. Again, I said yes.

"How much do you charge?" the venue owner asked me.

Keep in mind, at this point, I was just a dumb kid with

multiple jobs: the drive-through at Wendy's and working as an overnight janitor at Target. Not exactly fun jobs.

I told the owner I charged $200 an hour. In 1989, $200 an hour to fix audio gear was a crazy amount of money, but the owner said yes. That's when I knew working for someone else was not my cup of tea. I was going to run my own business for the rest of my life.

My first startup focused on—guess what?—fixing sound systems, and we grew that into a company that worked tours for rock-and-roll and country bands, many of which are household names: Nine Inch Nails, Metallica, B.B. King, Garth Brooks, and Pantera. I sold that company when I discovered the Internet and decided to start making software.

My first introduction to the Internet was in the early nineties. There was a coffee shop that had this clunky, old, beige computer that was connected to the Internet, which offered a handful of websites. There was no Google or Amazon. Yahoo barely existed.

People kept asking me if the Internet was cool. When I said it was, they asked how to build websites. Those conversations got me started making websites, and eventually that evolved into a software company called Coffee Cup that made the software that made websites.

Coffee Cup was my second startup, so named because it was started in the back of that coffee shop. It was one of the first HTML editors ever and some of the first shareware that ever existed. Shareware allows people to use a piece of software for a limited amount of time for free, and then they pay if they wish to continue using the software.

I was with Coffee Cup for fourteen years, and during that time, we created about sixty pieces of software for Windows, Mac, and the web. We also created a web hosting company that grew to about 25,000 hosted customers in less than two years. We sold the hosting company in 2002 and later sold Coffee Cup in two chunks to a Dutch investment firm.

When I moved to Atlanta in 2008, I was eager to find a community of web developers and designers, and I was surprised that not much of a community existed. So I helped create the Atlanta Web Design Group, which is now the leading organization of web professionals in the greater Atlanta area. This was my third startup.

After leaving the software business, I took a three-month vacation to figure out what I wanted to do next. I was already involved with the Atlanta Web Design Group during that time, so I had tons of professionals coming to me and asking how to solve certain problems, usually around building software and other digital products people wanted to buy. I started charging them to answer their questions, and that's how I became a consultant.

From there, I built Nine Labs (my fourth startup) into the consulting firm it is today. This book is a culmination of everything I've learned over my twenty-five-year career.

My fifth startup was a digital native vertical brand. Terminus Threads took discarded cloth from high-fashion companies and upcycled it into pocket squares. Ultimately, that business didn't work. Not all ideas turn into profitable businesses. I know this from experience!

When I started the sound system business decades ago, I dropped out of high school and never want back. I don't have a high school diploma, much less a college degree. Everything I've learned has come from building software and starting companies. That's my education. I don't really have those letters-beside-your-name qualifications some people look for, but I do have twenty-five years of experience building successful companies. That said, I recently completed classes at Wharton Business School to broaden my knowledge base.

I live in Atlanta, Georgia, with my wife, three kids, and two dogs. You can learn more about Nine Labs and our work at NineLabs.com. My personal website is JCornelius.com.

For all things book related, check out Loopsbook.com.

Made in the USA
Columbia, SC
28 August 2019